I0450014

IBB – Smart But Foolish

REASONS HE CAN'T BE THE NEXT PRESIDENT

By

Abejide Olusegun

Order this book online at www.trafford.com
or email orders@trafford.com

Most Trafford titles are also available at major online book retailers.

© Copyright 2010 Abejide Olusegun.
All rights reserved. No part of this publication may be reproduced, stored in a retrieval
system, or transmitted, in any form or by any means, electronic, mechanical, photocopying,
recording, or otherwise, without the written prior permission of the author.

Printed in the United States of America.

ISBN: 978-1-4269-4508-3 (sc)
ISBN: 978-1-4269-4509-0 (hc)
ISBN: 978-1-4269-4510-6 (e)

Library of Congress Control Number: 2010914488

*Our mission is to efficiently provide the world's finest, most comprehensive book publishing
service, enabling every author to experience success. To find out how to publish your book,
your way, and have it available worldwide, visit us online at www.trafford.com*

Trafford rev. 11/05/2010

 www.trafford.com

North America & international
toll-free: 1 888 232 4444 (USA & Canada)
phone: 250 383 6864 ♦ fax: 812 355 4082

For my loving daughter
Eniola Naomi

Alade Goldenpen,Hassan Aloma, Segun Bishop, Taiwo Omole and Rhosettie Abejide, without these people, this book wouldn't be completed. They are real patriotic Nigerians.

FOREWARD

NIGERIANS BEWARE: SLAVERY BECKONS

It is not a secret that it took the sweats of our heroes past to deliver this country from the grip of the colonial masters whom were more than determine to milk her to the end. After several failed suppression and procrastination, the country attained independence in 1960 and not until 1963 before it became a republic. Obviously the colonial masters were not happy with her independence; they rather preferred a stooge than the radical minded nationalists willing to take the nation forward. They stopped all those they knew will not play game with them from attaining the highest political offices.

And fifty years after independence, the Western world are still more interested in our resources than our development. They want our oil, they want our land and if possible our lives to satisfy their inordinate ambition. Unfortunately as the Nation is, we have been unable to have the right leaders to take us away from the grip of the Americans; the few that had tried, were either ursurped or killed.

The millions of Nigerian workers, youths, and peasants who raised the banner of freedom, anti-colonialism and self government-- the Zikists, Aminu Kanoists and Awoists-- would be disenchanted with present-day Nigeria. Will they not question the rationale for which Nigerian land, farmed by the Kwara peasantry was appropriated and given to white racists booted out of Zimbabwe and resettled in Nigeria? This neocolonial act was accommodated by the past foreign minister, Ojo Maduekwe, with his Hobbsian "Do-me-I-do-you" philosophy. An economic postulate was erected that the new white settlers will develop the nation's agriculture, and turn Nigeria into a food basket for Africa, as Saraki and Obasanjo were commended for their foresight. No thoughts were given to the settler's proven racist demeanors applied to enslave millions of Zimbabwean peasants who worked the land for them under the scorching sun with subsisting wages while they sat lazily under trees with their riffle, chewing tobacco, sure of their profit. No thought that history may again repeat itself.

Would not the heroic Muritala Ramat Mohammed who captured the nation's revolutionary mood and won for Nigeria the honorary recognition as a frontline state in the liberation of Angola, Zimbabwe, Namibia and South Africa have insisted that Britain should accept the responsibility to settle her former subjects? Under Obasanjo's first and second coming, the nation lost its non-alignment trajectory and was seduced into receiving orders to anchor Western interests from London or Washington.

Again the manifestation of neocolonialism is brazenly evident in the complete and shameless surrender to imperialism of the nation's economy. Not only does the World Bank and the International Monetary Fund manipulate the economy, Nigeria's former minister of finance as well as its former Central Bank Governor was both senior employees of these important Western finance institutions. Through these local agents, irreversible efforts were made to privatize all national institutions and branches of the Nigerian economy. Stock marketing, shareholder resorts, speculations and gambling, became entrenched and managed by the Nigerian Stock Exchange. The nation's currency, were devalued and banks reorganized into bigger conglomerates to allow for more efficient, exploitation by bigger finance-capital. The overall effort was to encourage an emergent stable middle class, from a polarized society of the few super rich against its majority of poor people, and postpone a social revolution. *One is then tempted to questions the hypocrisy of President Obama who had blamed Nigeria's backwardness as a result of its failure to build lasting institutions when the World Bank and IMF had prescribed the privatization of our national institutions, cuts in the funding of education and other welfare programs and the sales of our refineries and other agencies to the sleaziest bidder.*

A clear painful case of neocolonialism is also the present romance between the U. S. president through his top emissaries to Nigeria's former IMF client and military president, General Ibrahim Babangida, with the approaching national election. Of what sagacity does he engage in such rapport if not to display arrogance and disrespect for the Nigerian people who still bleed from the wounds inflicted by the dictator through his IMF directed Structural Adjustment Program? True, Babangida had once held the Nigerian state firmly in the armpit of the West during the cold war over communism, and proven to be a trusted friend. Then, the Mobutus, Savimbis and Babangidas headed military dictatorships throughout Africa as a Western strategy in Africa to contain social revolts that may become infected by Soviet communism. **With the present hiccups of capitalism, Babangida is appearing once more as an attractive bride to temper Washington's paranoia over Chinese communism**. Thus Abuja has been host for both former U. S. Secretary of State Condolizza Rice and even former U. S. president George W. Bush Jnr. within the last few months. Also Under- Secretary Johnny Carson has also brought good tidings to the General, with Babangida now declaring his intent to return to power.

How would the late Beko Ransome Kutis, the Chima Ubanis and the thousands of our unknown but heroic youths and workers who stood before tanks and machine guns in the streets of Lagos and Abuja to Campaign for Democracy and an end to military rule view the General's return to power in any capacity? How would the nation live with the imposition- by hook or crook- of the man who annulled the famous June 12th election and prolonged the struggle of the people for democratic rule? Even the role of Nigeria's military in Africa is clearly tempered by neocolonialism. The training of a substantial percentage of the officers of its air land and sea forces, as well as the mindset of these officers are jointly coordinated with the U. S. command. Its pan African duty to lead a fraternal alliance of West African states, to defend the Gulf of Guinea and secure our natural resources have been infiltrated under the subterfuge of cooperation. The nation and the world were recently informed by Admiral Mark Fitzgerald who commands U. S. Naval forces in Europe and Africa that America's interest in the Gulf of Guinea "is not just about oil but that illegal fishing and drug problems could destabilize the countries". Building up the capacities and capabilities of the local navies of course is a way of capturing the region under U. S. hegemony, without invitation by the Nigerian people. Also Nigerians do not want any super-power struggle near our shores.

Not only are the Nigerian Armed Forces used by imperialism to secure its short and long term interest in Africa, its Rapid Deployment Force and hopeful African Command, they also play security neocolonial roles to protect the interest of foreign multinational oil firms against the Nigerian people. The use of the military to subjugate the Ogoni people in the interest of Shell is a regular occurrence in Ogoni land. Indeed the recent uprising by native militants in the Niger Delta due to the destruction of their means of subsistence with its unparalleled poverty again required the Nigerian military to protect the oil installations of the multinational firms against its people. Under a policy of non alignment Muritala Mohammed created security agencies to monitor these foreign oil firms and not to kill the people. Under a foreign policy of neocolonialism on the other hand, the people are killed to protect the foreign oil firms and their profits.

Here then is a black nation- the most populous black nation on earth. Guided by its Pan African ideals a large population and a reasonable sized educated workforce, it is in essence the manifestation of a formidable Black Power. It is the answer to Marcus Garvey's quest for a government that is not just a democracy, but the Black man's government with its committed scientists, "Navy and men of big affairs" that will manifest the industrious intelligence of black people; a government that will lay the scientific foundations to protect black people against disease and poverty; one whose statistics we can truly rely on; a government that will be the pride of every black person, from the Americas to the Delta; fight against racism, economic exploitation and all forms of super power aggression against black people. These noble ideals can only be actualized through a foreign policy of non alignment. Then and only then will the call of great Garvey now heard only by few, echo within each African: "Up you mighty race, you can accomplish what you will!"
Nigerians let rise against this move; else we get ready for slavery in our fatherland.

CHAPTER ONE
Is Obama romancing Ibrahim Babangida?

Democracy opens new vistas and opportunities. We should use the opportunities it offers to correct past mistakes not to blunder anew.

Ibrahim Babangida

February 10, 2010, the Barack Obama administration made a move that's likely to hurt its credibility among Nigerians. Johnnie Carson, the United States Assistant Secretary of State for African Affairs, and Robin Sanders, the US Ambassador to Nigeria, traveled to Minna to confer with former Nigerian dictator, Ibrahim Babangida, at his hilltop mansion. That visit was, I suggest, a serious diplomatic gaffe – and one unworthy of the Obama administration.

That neither the American diplomats nor Babangida disclosed the subject of the meeting compounded the gravity of the misstep. For one, it raised speculation that the US government wanted to signal its tacit support for Babangida's run for the presidency in next year's elections. At the very least, the parley suggested that Obama's team regards the retired general as an instrument for solving Nigeria's myriad, and deep, political crises. Either goal represents a serious lapse in judgment on the part of the Obama administration.

And the visit brings to question the true reflection of America's policy towards Africa. In an interview in 2007, Senator Uba Ahmed alleged that the acclaimed world number one nation has always wanted the backwardness of the giant of Africa. According to him, "the issue of the value of our currency lies at the centre of our political crisis. As far back as 1982, the US government under President Ronald Regan asked the Shehu Shagari government to devalue the Naira by a whopping 500%. Shagari refused on the ground that the measure would impoverish Nigerians. He said it would be suicidal for his government to accept that when the Nigerian economy hasn't got the capacity to raise its production by a corresponding 500%. If he had accepted that request from Reagan under the prevailing economic situation at the time, Nigerians would have been impoverished by over 500%".

He added that the decline did not go well with Reagan who then "threatened our government and warned of dire consequences. A lot of arm-twisting economic measures against Nigeria followed from then on. Even the British under Margaret Thatcher joined the Americans. He said that in March, 1983, Nigerian suddenly woke up that morning and heard that all the buyers of Nigerian oil from Western countries were no more interested in Nigerian oil as sweet as it were and being the best oil available in market.

It was a natural shock to all of Nigerians. We had to stampede President Shagari and take him to the Senate to go over and to within 24 hours to make what we called Economic Stability Act. The government therefore imposed import duties, et cetera, moderately so that we will be able to accommodate the intervening period of loss of sales and loss of export of oil until the OPEC which realised with our failure to export oil, OPEC as an organisation will beckon. So they collected two billion dollars to come to our aid".

The help that OPEC promised was a burden to America as "Reagan took his phone and called King Fahd of Saudi Arabia and said it will be against the interest of America if the OPEC and the Arab countries were to come to the aid of Nigeria with 2 billion dollars. Thus, that kind of amount of money was drastically reduced to 700 million dollars because the OPEC countries were determined to come to our aid and it was Gadafi that brought the cash personally because they couldn't do it through the normal banking transactions in-case the American government will trace it. So since we did not budge to depreciate our naira the way they wanted it we were overthrown by their boys the way he said it".

This is a true reflection of the view shared by many that every coup that has taken place in the country has been sponsored by the America for their selfish interest, and unfortunately, IBB is one man that has been fingered in successive coup in the country-a true son of our imperial lord.

It should also be noted that the America-finacied IMF which has in more than one way impoverished the economy of Nigeria and other 'third world nations'(as they made us to belief we are). According to Daily Independent Online (22/4/06), Nigeria on October 31, 2005 "paid $6 billion arrears of debt it owed Paris Club of creditors and that marked the commencement of the eventual liquidation of the remaining $12.4 billion left of the $36 billion debt after the forgiveness of $18 billion debt, under the Naples Terms." Sources acquainted with the subject of Nigeria's external debt state that in actual fact Nigeria borrowed less than $10 billion dollars, but due to interest charges and penalty for not paying on schedule, including "penalty for the penalty," it paid $35 billion over 20 years and still owed $30 billion as at 2004 and later $36 billion before receiving the debt forgiveness of $18 billion which helped in our exit from the hell of debt, as it gradually cleared the remaining balance.

Babngida relationship could be traced to early 1980s when he was sent to U.S in 1983, for a military course, during the Reagan administration. He admired Ronald Reagan's Machiavellian dribbles with the American public and became a disciple of Reagan's trickle-down economics, popularly derided as "voodoo" economics, where the resources and wealth of a nation are distributed to a few cronies, with the hope that their business activities would create wealth that would trickle down to the common man! This is how Babangida single-handedly wiped out the Nigerian middle class, creating a few stealing billionaires and a mass of poverty, with nothing in-between.

Anyway, while in the U.S. it became obvious that Babangida was recruited by the CIA. Mobutu's power and relevance to the U.S interests in Africa was waning and they needed another Mobutu in a strategic country. Babangida fitted Mobutu's personality traits; very ambitious, unpatriotic, bold, greedy and cunning. So Babangida fitted the profile of a strong-man, like Mobutu, the U.S was looking for.

3

It should be remember that it was also during this period that Reagan was fighting several covert or proxy wars around the world. The war between U.S and Nicaragua is an example of such war. When Daniel Ortega of Nicaragua became the leader of that country, it did not go well with America because of his Marxit Leaning stye. Because of this , Us went into war with him. US congress was kept in the dark as they continue funding the war.. But when it came to their knowledge, they cut off all funding for the illegal war. Since CIA determined bring Ortega's government down by all possible means, they came up with selling illegal drug. They could not do this from the U.S soil, so they look for a Third World country to import the hard drugs and later smuggle to the U.S. Nigeria was the best country to them. Hence, to overthrone the Buhari/ Idiagbon gorvernment will be the best since the regim was a pathrotic one and saw how its was killing any body cached with any hard drugs.

Here comes Babangida and the coup that overthrew Buhari regime, covertly planned and supported and carried out with the aid of the CIA. As soon as Babangida came to power, he undo everything the Buhari regime tried to achieved for a better Nigeria. After this, the CIA cut a deal with Babangida, where Nigeria was used as a major drug transit and money laundering center for the proceeds of the CIA drug trade. This is how the CIA was funding their Contra war. Two investigative journalists in the US later broke the news that the CIA was involved in drug smuggling to fund the Contra War. They didn't mention the country that was used, but from all indications, it was Nigeria! However, Dele Giwa somehow stumbled on this information and was seriously investigating it and was about to break the news when he was killed. This is one of the main reason that Babangida had Dele Giwa killed. Now the CIA want him back.

After the former leader of Burkina Faso, Capt. Thomas Sankara was killed, obviously with help from the West; the rest of Africa condemned the cowardly act except Babangida. As a matter of fact, he gave the leader of the coup that killed Sankara, Major Compaore Blaise, a red carpet welcome to Lagos, barely a week after the murder. Again when in 1986, Reagan unjustifiably bombed Libya and killed Gadaffi's daughter, everybody in Africa condemned the unprovoked attack, except Babangida, who was blaming Gaddafi for the attack. Toward the end of 1986, or 1987, Babangida was given a "Strategic" award, by the Heritage Foundation, a US right wing front whose philosophy is total world domination, economically, politically and militarily. The few other people, who had received this award, include Henry Kissinger and the former NATO Commander, Alexander Haig, people who had gone out of their way and the risk of their lives to advance America's interests.

It would appear that Babangida covets the Nigerian presidency. Four years ago, he and his cohorts orchestrated what was tagged Project 007, implying that the former military head of state considered himself a shoe-in as President Olusegun Obasanjo's successor. Nigerians, for understandable reasons, were disquieted by the prospect of another IBB presidency. Many heaved a sigh of relief when Obasanjo, for reasons hard to fathom, foiled Babangida's ambition.

There's no question: Babangida is one of the most enigmatic figures to have emerged in Nigerian politics. I have always found the man intriguing, but in a sad, even tragic sort of way. In 1993, Babangida lost power in one of his costly, purposeless gambles. His annulment of the June 12 election, an act of supreme perfidy, precipitated his own political downfall. In characteristic fashion, he euphemized his fall from power as a decision to "step aside."

One hopes that the Obama who went to Accra and spoke eloquently about Nigeria's leadership crisis has not permitted himself to be led into the contradiction of prescribing IBB as the answer. Or even as a factor in finding the answer to Nigeria's quagmire.

Obama must guard against the Bill Clinton error. Even though former President Clinton is popular in Nigeria, many Nigerians are still appalled by his bizarre statement, in the heydays of Sani Abacha's self-succession plan, that the US was open to recognizing the bespectacled dictator if he won an election. That statement came at a time when any neophyte knew that Abacha didn't plan to hold a credible election. In making such a public show of coddling Babangida, the Obama administration risked being perceived as wishing to forestall the ongoing mobilization of a progressive force to serve as a viable alternative to the grubby, visionless elements that have steered Nigeria to perilous waters.

If Washington doesn't want to see a cataclysm befall Nigeria, with horrible consequences for Nigerians and the international community, then it must rethink its seeming courtship with the Babangidas of Nigeria.

CHAPTER TWO
Who Is Babangida?

Ibrahim Badamasi Babangida, a.k.a, IBB, is popularly called Maradona by Nigerians for his special skill to cheat and divert, in the fashion of Argentina's soccer genius, Diego Maradona, who infamously cheated to earn victory over England in the 1986 World Cup. A self-described 'evil genius,' Babangida led Nigerians through a tortuous and deceptive political and economic transition that ended in a cul-de-sac. Perhaps because of his craftiness, it wasn't until the end of his military career that the dictator's ruthlessness and lust for power became obvious.

He is believed to have been born August 17, 1941, at Minna, Niger State. This man is not regarded as a true northerner from Nigeria. In the northern part of Nigeria, there is this muted discussion about General Ibrahim Babangida not being a Nigerian but from Niger Republic who was not regarded much until he agreed to join the army and was greatly encouraged by the oligarchy who demanded one thing from him, the institution of Islamic regime in Nigeria. He does not care much about anything unless it means power and control under his watch. He stepped aside and ever since, he has always being in the aside deciding how the people are controlled using military and civilians.

He attended Government College, Bida, from 1957 to 1962. There is no evidence he passed his School Certificate examination, as he did not receive his undisclosed results until three decades later in a publicized ceremony as the military head of state. Babangida received his military training at the Nigerian Military College, Kaduna, and was commissioned into the Nigerian Army as a 2nd Lieutenant in 1963, just like many of his colleagues, some of whom could not demonstrate the measure of literacy expected of an officer.

He was given further military training at Nigeria's expense, which he paid back by way of incessant coup plots. Judging by his records, Babangida seemed more interested in politics than a professional military career, as he had been the face behind every military coup in Nigeria over a 30-year period. It is not a secret, and the BBC remarks, that Babangida had taken part in all coups in Nigeria. With his cohorts, he unleashed many years of needless bloodshed and power rotation that left Africa's highest grossing nation one of its poorest.

When the military returned to power December 30, 1983, IBB became the chief of army staff and member of the highest ruling military body, the Supreme Military Council, SMC. He also served in that council during the Murtala Muhammed/Olusegun Obasanjo administration. On August 27, 1985, the Muhammadu Buhari/Tunde Idiagbon administration was toppled in a palace coup by Babangida, who understandably made himself Nigeria's first "military President," an indication of his lust for political power. Babangida was Nigeria's sixth military ruler and inarguably the most powerful.

IBB has received numerous national and military decorations, most of which he awarded himself or received from his subordinates and beneficiaries. To his supporters, he is a god - because he showered them with material benefits, stolen from the national treasury. However, to most Nigerians, he remains a brutal dictator, much disliked by the millions of Nigerians whose hopes and dreams IBB's evil orchestrations over the years have helped to truncate. But apparently this menace to the society has been well shielded from justice, supposedly by the current political dispensation and he yet wields enough corrupt influence to try to buy his way around millions of hungry Nigerians. Babangida now hides most of the time in his vast and opulent 50-room mansion in his hometown of Minna because he knows it could be fatal for him to venture out. He has been attacked in public before, and fears some angry Nigerians could maul him on the street.

Married with four children, Babangida said his hobbies are reading (he has not written a book, not even a newspaper article, to date), listening to people and their problems (he has created more political and economic problems for Nigeria than any other military ruler), and sports. As with most dictators, the evil genius was methodical, shrewd in power, flamboyant in style, and ruthless in response. His predecessor, Mohammadu Buhari was resolute, but Babangida would kill by any means necessary and would not consider it inappropriate to weep at his enemy's funeral.

Deft and tactical, Babangida announced himself to power as a champion of human rights, but unleashed a spate of human rights abuses that was only matched by his savage successor, Sani Abacha. As he strategically spread his political tentacles, Maradona's first call was to release most of those jailed by Buhari, including the late music star, Fela Kuti. Nonetheless, Babangida brutally muffled opposition, as he frequently detained labor leaders, students and human rights advocates. The man who adopted the title"president" behaved more like a politician than a soldier while ruling as a dictator.

Ibrahim Babangida has been indicted by the Human Rights Violations Investigation Commission, led by the respected Justice Chukwudifu Oputa, for the killing of Nigeria's top journalist, Mr. Dele Giwa, by a parcel bomb in 1986. Up till now, the killers of Dele Giwa have not been officially exposed, and efforts to probe Babangida's implicated associates have been consistently blocked by him. The report noted: "On General Ibrahim Babangida, we are of the view that there is evidence to suggest that he and the two security chiefs, Brigadier General Halilu Akilu and Col. A. K. Togun are accountable for the death of Dele Giwa by letter bomb. We recommend that this case be re-open for further investigation in the public interest." Babangida has blocked that report from being released through the judicial system he blatantly corrupted.

By the time Babangida was one year in power, he had begun to demonstrate his deceptive abilities. He started a national debate on whether to accept an International Monetary Fund (IMF) loan or embark on austerity measures. Thinking their leader was faithful, Nigerians favored the measures but soon found that the Structural Adjustment Program (SAP) was not being faithfully executed. While they were sacrificing, billions of dollars of

Nigeria's money was being pocketed by Babangida and his followers, such that under SAP, unemployment numbers, food prices, and cost of living soared. While Ghana and Uganda were making gains under SAP, Nigeria was going under, until Nigerians responded in a 1989 riot, to which the dictator replied by first killing hundreds of protesters, then issuing palliative measures. A World Bank report issued in 1995 fully documented how grand theft under Babangida's regime nullified the gains of SAP. His government implemented a myriad of failed programs, which only helped to divert attention and fritter scarce national resources. Such programs include the People's Bank, Directorate of Food, Roads and Rural Infrastructure (DFRRI), National Directorate of Employment (NDE), and Better Life for Rural Women. All these programs are today moribund or dead.

Among his other deceptive ways, Babangida replaced his deputy, Commodore Ebitu Ukiwe with Rear Admiral Augustus Aikhomu. The former was headstrong and idealistic, while the later was largely a yes-man. He executed dramatic changes in public administration, filling strategic military and ministerial positions with his loyalists. The headship of the ministries of external affairs, petroleum resources, internal affairs and agriculture, considered the most powerful cabinet posts, were awarded by ethnic parameters. Babangida introduced measures that threatened the secularity of Nigeria. Under his watch, Nigeria secretly became a participant at the Organization of the Islamic Conference (OIC), an action so controversial that it was linked to the ouster of Ebitu Ukiwe.

As things got worse, a band of top officers, including Babangida's colleague and best man at his wedding, General Mamman Vatsa, allegedly planned to remove him. They were all captured and killed without sufficient evidence. We now know in 2006 that Vatsa may have been murdered for offences he did not commit, going by revelations by the former Chief of Defence Staff, General Domkat Bali.

Nigeria continued in spiral fall until April 22, 1990, when a brave junior officer, Major Gideon Orkar, almost toppled the Babangida regime. The official residence of the head of state, the Dodan Barracks, was razed. Babangida escaped by a slim stroke of luck. Significantly, Nigerian civilians were, for the first time, involved in a coup attempt, a development the dictator responded to by quickly moving the seat of power from the heavily populated Lagos to previously abandoned national capital city of Abuja, just about an hour's drive from his hometown. Orkar had, however, made damaging allegations about Babangida's personal life and political problems, including homosexuality, drug peddling and corruption.

From this point, IBB was held in widespread suspicion among Nigerians. He held on to power with a single promise: to lead Nigeria back to democracy. Trusting and hopeful once again, Nigerians were carried along until 1992, when his abrupt cancellation of a political process led to mass suspicion about his true intentions. At this point, the term "Hidden Agenda" was coined by the late lawyer, Mr. Alao Aka Bashorun, who declared that Babangida was attempting to succeed himself. Bashorun seemed to have provided light in a dark tunnel as Nigerians began to place the evil genius' programs under the microscope.

The outcry that followed the cancellation of presidential primaries about to be won by the late General Shehu Yar'Adua led Babangida to hurriedly, without much of his usual plotting, move the political transition process at such a pace that caused a generally accepted candidate, billionaire philanthropist, M.K.O Abiola, to be elected as president in Nigeria's most peaceful and acceptable election. Confused and dazed, IBB annulled that election and unleashed a national outrage that led to his downfall. Hundreds of Nigerians were killed by soldiers acting under the directives of Babangida and his beneficiaries, as the citizens fought for the mandate given to Abiola.

Eventually, it dawned on the Maradona, the game was up. He was forced to vacate his beloved presidential seat. Nigerians can remember how Babangida made a spectacle of himself on the NTA as he bounced continuously on a chair in utter confusion when he had to "step aside." Babangida was forced out, but not before he planted his equally ruthless and utterly vindictive partner, the late General Sani Abacha, to guide a lame civilian caretaker administration of Ernest Shonekan. It surprised no one that Abacha sent Shonekan packing in less than three months, and continued the evil legacy of his former boss, IBB.

The hand of God played Abacha out (or so people think), as he died mysteriously in power. Strangely, other leaders, including M.K.O Abiola and General Tunde Idiagbon died in the same manner, all in Abuja, within

11

months of each other. Babangida's crony and kinsman, General Abubakar Abdulsalam, became the Head of State overnight. The stage was set for Babangida's return to the limelight, as he quickly arranged for former military head of state, General Olusegun Obasanjo, to assume power as civilian president. Obasanjo was probably the guinea pig for Babangida's experimentation of former military ruler as civilian president. Nigerians have responded favorably to Babangida's experiment, having accepted Obasanjo, also a former soldier.

The bedrock for today's economic and financial problems in Nigeria was laid by this man, Ibrahim Babangida! He created conditions malignant to national advancement, such as the institutionalization of the culture of corruption that is now heavily entrenched in the social and moral fabric of the Nigerian society. The phenomena of the notorious thievery schemes or theft-by-deception, a.k.a "419," is largely believed to have gained undue prominence and seeming acceptance during the eight-year misrule of Ibrahim Babangida in Nigeria. Today, the nuisance of the so-called "Yahoo Boys" is believed to be a by-product or creation of the IBB era. What is the moral justification for a society to wage war on scammers when known social culprits enjoy stolen public wealth without restraint? These conditions have been almost impossible to reverse. And now, IBB is out again to try to make vain the labors of our heroes past.

Cozie Chimason, a Nigerian based in the United States of America has opined in an article posted by Akintokunbo Adejumo on April 13, 2010 that, "the sole architect of the extreme corruption as seen today in Nigeria and the sorry state of affairs is no other than the former dictator, IBRAHIM BADAMOSI BABANGIDA. According to him, one of IBB relatives was his roommate in the US during his under graduate education. He was able to glimpse the true nature of the beast from him. Here is the Babangida most Nigerians know nothing about. Babangida is the most destabilizing force in Nigeria today and the more Nigerians know about it the better", adding that, "his cousin had described him to him, as a ruthless, vindictive, unforgiving megalomaniac and extremely corrupt. Since he literally determines what happens in Nigeria, it might be very dangerous to pose a frontal attack against him. He's a very ruthless man and powerful. If he could order his childhood friend, Gen. Mamman Vatsa, to be killed without batting an eyelid, we'd be just small mosquitoes! Babangida remains the most destabilizing and powerful force in Nigeria today. It's almost as if he owns Nigeria. He remains untouchable because most of the recycled kleptomaniacs called politicians, who are in leadership positions today, owe their wealth and power to Babangida".

For the eight years he stayed in office, dishonesty and corruption were elevated to the level of state policy. Many times, Babangida critics have said that anybody who is careless around the man does so at his own peril. **"Anybody who has Babangida as a friend does not need an enemy,"** sang the late Moshood Kashomawo Olawale Abiola, after IBB annulled the June 12, 1993 presidential election he (Abiola) won.

CHAPTER THREE
IBB and June 12

This man is behind the annulment of the only election that most of us ever voted for in Nigeria. He made it impossible for MKO Abiola, that man whose election brought down prices of staple food, but was truncated due to power play championed by Babangida The oligarchy did not trust Abiola that he will be true to his muslim beliefs once in office and they had to go through Babangida to stop him. He canceled the election and almost plunged the country into civil war. Many people died in the roads of Nigeria as they were rushing back to their states of origin. He caused the death of very many people in all the western states of Nigeria including those that were killed at University of Lagos.

Speaking obliquely a few months ago in Babangidaspeak, he threatened that when he would speak on the June 12 annulment issue, Nigeria would shake to her foundations. In an interview in late May, 2004, on Channels TV, Babangida spoke on the June 12 issue, and no feathers were ruffled. Instead, Babangida admitted toothy smile and all, that he made a mistake but that he did it in the interest of Nigeria

Four years into his regime in 1989, he lifted for the first time his ban on partisan politics, and set up two political parastatals. One was called the Social Democratic Party (SDP), and the other was the National Republican Convention (NRC).

The handing over date to civilian government was postponed once again from late 1990 to the 1st of October 1992. He allowed elections to be held into the local governments in 1990, and in 1991, Babangida instigated intra party squabbles to find excuse to ban 12 of the candidates participating in the governorship elections. Candidates replacing the disqualified ones had barely one week to campaign.

Elections into the State Assemblies miraculously held without too much acrimony, followed shortly afterwards by elections into the National Assembly. In all the elections, known individuals strongly against Babangida or the military in power were sidelined, banned, or hounded into exile, prominent among whom were Ibrahim Tahir of the NPN, Sam Mbakwe, Chris Okolie, Wahab Dosumu, Ebenezer Babatope, etc.

Allegation of massive rigging was invoked on 17 November, 1992, to ban Adamu Ciroma and Shehu Musa Yar Adua, who had emerged from party primaries as presidential candidates for the NRC and the SDP respectively, and 21 other presidential aspirants, (including Chief Arthur Nzeribe, Chief Olu Falae, Alhaji Lateef Jakande and Alhaji Umar Shinkafi), from participating in the scheduled August 1992 presidential election, and all other future elections. The trick was that Babangida was gradually narrowing the field of potential presidential materials to himself. Remember that Babangida had promised Yar Adua the Presidency when Yar Adua helped to actualize the 1985 coup that brought Babangida to power. The ban did not go down well with the political elite in general, and particularly with Yar Adua who had assumed he would take over leadership from Babangida.

With the ban, Babangida once again postponed his handing over date from October 1st 1992, to Dec 5, 1992. Soon after, Babangida mandated the National Electoral Commission (NEC), to conduct the presidential primaries of the political parties, and he again fixed a new date of January 3, 1993, for the handing over of the reigns of power to a civilian government. Bribery, thuggery, rigging, ethnic cleavages, etc., ruined the NEC supervised political parties' presidential primaries, resulting in the dissolution of party executives, who were replaced by Sole Administrators, and National Coordinators. Handing over date was once again postponed to August 27, 1993.

Baba Gana Kingibe, who was the SDP chairman before the dissolution of the party executives, and was then supposed to be managing the affairs of

Yar Adua, was alleged to have received Babangida's backing and financial support to aspire as presidential candidate obviously to cause confusion in Yar Adua's political camp. Kingibe pasted his campaign posters all over the place, causing bad blood between himself and Yar Adua, which spilled into the Jos SDP convention of 1993.

In the meantime, Babangida was busy creating anarchy in the ranks of the politicians by introducing his modified open ballot system, and insisting that presidential aspirants go through tedious ward, local government, and state congresses. This eventually produced two presidential aspirants for each of the states, plus two for the FCT, and the unwieldy 62 presidential aspirants had to go through further elimination processes, at various national congresses, before the Jos (SDP), and Port-Harcourt (NRC), conventions of 1993. Several irregularities were observed at the party conventions and a lot of money changed hands.

Alhaji Bashir Tofa for the NRC, and Bashorun M.K.O Abiola for the SDP, emerged as the presidential flag bearers. Babangida who was unhappy that progress was being made in the presidential election process was further pissed-off when his nominee, Pascal Bafyau, the ex-NLC president, as Abiola's running mate, (to spy on and undermine Abiola), was rejected by Abiola. Abiola also upset Yar Adua's calculations, by not accepting Abubakir Atiku as his running mate, and choosing Baba Gana Kingibe instead.

Of course, the emergence at last of promising presidential candidates for both parties was not a very palatable option for Abacha too who was still nursing the dream to succeed Babangida although pretending to be on the side of Babangida. Abacha misled Babangida to think of him as a possible ally, so the scene was set for Babangida to feel that if he annulled the election, he would have the support of Abacha, Yar Adua and other perceived, powerful enemies of Abiola, including a leading traditional ruler in the South-West.

Babangida, in his determination to scuttle the presidential election at all cost, promulgated Decree 13, forbidding the presidential flag bearers of the two political parties from doing anything whatsoever that would influence members of the public to vote for them at the election scheduled for June 12 1993. Then Babangida empowered NEC to disqualify any of the candidates at will, and as a (final) fall back strategy, to scuttle our democratic dream, he set up his Association for Better Nigeria (ABN) party, using Senator Arthur Nzeribe as proxy.

On June 10, 1993, at the unholy hour of 9.30 pm, late Justice Ikpeme, who was appointed a few days earlier and hurriedly transferred from Lagos to Abuja, granted a court order to the ABN, restraining the NEC Chairman Humphrey Nwosu, from conducting the Presidential election on June 12, 1993.

The Director of the United States Information Service (USIS) in Nigeria at the time, Mr. O'Brien, warned that the US government would not be happy if the June 12 election was cancelled. Babangida panicked, and although he declared O'Brien persona non grata and ordered him out of the country in his personal interest, Babangida allowed Nwosu to go ahead with the election.

The election was adjudged by the international and local observers monitoring it and by the two political parties involved, as the fairest and freest in the history of Nigeria. By the evening of June 14 1993, more than 50% of the election results had been authenticated and released by NEC, showing that SDP's Moshood Abiola had swept the polls.

To everyone's surprise, Babangida suddenly ordered NEC not to release any more results. On June 23, 1993, Babangida gave an unsigned statement to Nduka Irabor, his press secretary, announcing the cancellation of the presidential election on the radio. The unsigned statement was a strategy to allow Babangida to deny its authenticity, should Nigeria begin to boil over the announcement. Nigerians had become too hungry and docile to react.

Babangida annulled the June12 election entirely on his own, based on his selfish, personal agenda to rule indefinitely. Before annulling the election, he rallied the connivance and support of some critical Emirs and a leading Yoruba traditional ruler known to be antagonistic to Abiola's political ambition, and the signatures of a bunch of political and military apologists (or jobbers), tagged the G-34, on a document entitled 'Peace Pact,' in endorsement of his annulment of the June 12, 1993, elections.

The G-34 comprised of the following members of the military junta and leaders of the two political parties, the SDP and the NRC: Admiral Augustus Aikhomu, Chief Earnest Shonekan who eventually headed Babangida's contraption called the Interim National Government (ING), General Shehu Musa Yar'ardua, Alhaji Sule Lamido, Alhaji Adamu Ciroma, Amb. Dele Cole, Chief Tony Anenih, Chief Jim Nwobodo, Brig-Gen David A. B Mark, Alhaji Abubakar Rimi, Alhaji Olusola Saraki, Chief Dapo Sarumi, Chief Joseph Toba, Chief Bola Afonja, Dr. Hammed Kusamotu, Dr. Okechukwu Odunze, Prof. Eyo Ita, Y. Anka, Alhaji Bashir Dalhatu, Chief Tom Ikimi, Barrister Joe Nwodo (who signed with reservations), Dr. Bawa Salka, Alhaji Abba Murtala Mohammed, Alhaji Abdulrahman Okene, Lt. Gen Joshua Dongoyaro, Lt. Gen Aliyu Mohammed Gusau, Brig-Gen John Shagaya, Brig-Gen Anthony Ukpo, Halilu A. Maina, Alhaji Bawa Salka, Mr. Amos Idakula, Mr. Theo Nikire, Alhaji A. Ramalan, Alhaji A. Mohammed. Many of these traitors are still making decisions for Nigeria today.

Those who thought the outrage over the annulment of the June 12, 1993 election had been doused may be far from the reality, as Nigerians were admonished to vehemently resist Ibrahim Babangida, the dictator responsible for the scuttling of the polls described as the freest and fairest in the history of the country.

At the public presentation of a book, Diary of a Debacle: Tracking Nigeria's Failed Democratic Transition (1989-1994) some time back in Lagos former Chairman, Economic and Financial Crime Commission (EFCC) Mallam Nuhu Ribadu and erstwhile governor of Lagos State, Senator Bola Ahmed Tinubu were among those who called on every Nigerian and lovers of Nigeria to keep up the spirit of the June 12, 1993 election alive.
Ribadu, in his speech, described the annulment of June 12, 1993 election as a political corruption that deserves the prosecution of the perpetrators. He expressed concern that some of the principal actors of the dastardly act are at it again coming out and wanting to contest election in 2011. At this point, he called on all Nigerians who voted in support of June 12 to resist such people, saying they have nothing good to offer.

Ribadu said: "It is painful when we talk about June 12, 1993 election without reference to thousands of people who died during the struggle, yet those responsible for it are coming on board again. The act almost made the country went into extinction. Many people were returning to their regions, it created confusion in the nation."

The anti-corruption czar called on Nigerians to keep the spirit of June 12 election alive, saying "A new Nigeria is possible. It is very possible. We must all work in the spirit of June 12, 1993 election to keep the nation one and move it forward. It was a spirit of determination, a resolute and positive spirit. Although lives were lost, property destroyed and people suffered, but today, the same spirit bore us democracy and I belief it can also bring about new Nigeria."

CHAPTER FOUR
IBB and Murder

If the physical failed, the metaphysical was handy in the human blood bath for power. Blood was the language in the cultish game for total control. Fear gripped the land. Who was going to be the next victim? Life was scary and worthless. Corridor of power social acolytes of the time like the Arisekolas, Adedibus and the Akinyeles, could write blood-cuddling masterpieces on the mysteries of the season. Assassinations were rampant, sophisticated and comprehensive, incorporating bombings and dare-devil forages. Media houses were burnt or closed down, and critics of government were murdered, incarcerated or hounded into exile. Plane loads of promising young army officers lost their lives in questionable circumstances. Others appeared to have been sacrificed in distant land civil wars.

The Ejigbo military Hercules crash that killed an elite corp. of army captains and majors returning to their Jaji training base is a typical example of the terrible human carnage visited upon us at the time by a desperate tyrant bent on holding on to power indefinitely at all costs. The plane was doctored and it crashed a few seconds after take-off from the Murtala Mohammed airport. No rescue attempt was ordered or made until 24 hours after the crash and even then, the inadequate facilities of a private company, (Julius Berger), were relied upon. Forty-eight hours after the crash, a warm body was still found suggesting that some lives could have been saved if rescue operations had commenced minutes after the crash.

Apart from the needless assassinations of possible opponents and rivals for power, there were totally senseless ones too, such as the death of Murtala Mohammed's first son immediately after visiting the seat of power. It was generously reported in the press at the time. The allegation was that during the friendly, private visit, the young man was asked if he would be prepared to do a job. The young chap said he could not say until he was told what the job was. When told that he was to help facilitate the elimination of Chief Abiola, the young man said he couldn't because Abiola was like a father to him. The host then quickly dismissed the suggestion as if it had been a joke and asked how the young man travelled to the state house. "By private car," the young man said. "You are going about without security?" the host asked, pretending to look alarmed, and detailed some security officers to escort the young man to his Minna destination. The body of the young man was later that day found in his car on the route between the seat of power and Minna.

Bongos Ikwe's son by a girl friend, who later married late Maryam Babangida, also lost his life in suspicious circumstances. Bongos, in press interviews at the time, denied knowing his son's mother who, in fact, is the junior sister of Bongos' best friend and music partner on an RKTV programme in the early 60s. Despite denials, Bongos' most popular recorded song 'O Mariana' could not conceal the anguish of the jilted lover.

On why Babangida ignored all pleas not to kill Mamman Vasta, the master dribbler said that Vasta's death was a painful decision for him, but that he had no choice in the matter, because he was following military rules, and he did it in the national interest. But Vasta, his fellow infantry soldier and childhood friend, was hurriedly killed and his body dumped in a mass grave on the night of the announcement of his sentence, (i.e. early morning of 5th March 1986), to prevent last minute pleas for reprieve. Acid was poured on the bodies, including Vasta's and burnt, so one must ask, was the rush to kill Vasta and burn his carcass sanctioned too by the military laws? The whole thing smacks of envy, apart from being hideous and barbaric. Babangida used the phantom coup allegation to remove or marginalize the Middle Belt military top brass in his government.

Perhaps the most stupid, irresponsible and callous murder of them all was that of Dele Giwa. The death was a classic example of desperate, high-handed, dirty and mean under-the-carpet cover-up state terrorism.

Dele Giwa's problem was that he stumbled on some documents about Gloria Okon in London and after interviewing her, threatened to publish the story while allegedly letting it be known that he could be persuaded to withdraw publication with a cash bribe of US$21m plus N200m. Alternatively, he was ready to settle for the position of Information Minister, which Tony Mommoh was occupying at the time. Dele Giwa's blackmail unfortunately misfired unlike an earlier one involving Mr. Lawson, the founder of the Nigerian Grail Movement who was alleged to have been arrested and locked up in London for money laundering problems. Mudashiru, the military governor of Lagos state at the time of Lawson's travails, was alleged to have stopped the publication of Lawson's story by bribing Giwa with the land and C of O of the Newswatch plaza.

Babangida's boys went ahead to frame up Giwa anyway. Three days before they killed Dele Giwa, Col. A. K. Togun, the deputy Director of Babangida's State Security Service (the SSS), invited Giwa to his office and accused him of involvement in the importation of arms while linking Giwa with other persons alleged to be trying to stage a socialist revolution in Nigeria. At the meeting, agreement was reached, and Babangida, through his emissaries, promised to meet Giwa's terms. Two days before Giwa's murder, Akilu allegedly phoned Giwa's home to ask for direction because Babangida's ADC "has something for him, an invitation or something."

Dele Giwa allegedly invited the overseas editor of Newswatch at the time to be around. Obviously, Giwa took the president's promise more seriously than his colleagues at the Newswatch. This was why, when Giwa received the parcel and confirmed that it was from the President, his guest's first reaction was to dash off to take cover in the toilet adjacent to the room where Giwa opened the parcel bomb. The guest escaped death by the whiskers and blasted eardrums. Togun, when asked by Airport Correspondents on October 27, 1986, about Giwa's bombing inadvertently confirmed the blackmail reason for Giwa's death when he said: "We came to a real agreement and one person cannot just come out and blackmail us. I am an expert on blackmail. If a motorcycle man suddenly dashed in front of a car and the driver kills the motorcycle man, another motorcycle man who was there would not say the motorcycle man who dashed in front of the car was wrong. He would say the driver killed him, not that he killed himself"

An Arab terrorist, who was recruited to collaborate with a University of Ibadan chemistry don especially for the task, produced the bomb. The terrorist is alleged to have gone with Major Buba Marwa, Ogbeha and Gwazo, in a Peugeot station wagon car with fake license plate numbers, to deliver the bomb at Dele's home. On arrival, they were told that Dele was not in, so they laid ambush near-by to watch movements in and out of Giwa's premises. As soon as Giwa was spotted entering his house, the allegation continues, the Arab terrorist offered to go and deliver the bomb, but his colleagues in crime stopped him on the grounds that his color would look too suspicious for the job. Marwa, accompanied by Ogbeha, are alleged to have delivered the bomb to Dele's son at the door, after which the crime team drove off to Mafoluku where they burned their delivery car. The same day, the Arab terrorist was flown out of Lagos, first to Kano, and eventually out of the country.

We do not know if this was the reason. Someone also died around that time, Dan Archibong, Military Governor of Cross River State under Babangida. It was reported that he died in a car accident on his way back to Cross River. He was in Lagos on the invitation of the Military President Babangida. But we did not see the car that killed Archibong, was he driving alone at the time of the accident? Was it a collision of two cars? A governor under the military as we know it, travel with escorts but what happened to Archibong? He got killed on the Gloria Okon-related issue.

Odeleke, husband of Bola Odeleke the woman Bishop, until his death was a Colonel in the Nigerian Army, he was in Abuja to attend a meeting summoned by President Babangida, what we later heard was that, while on short break, Odeleke was killed by a hit-and-run car in Abuja, in day light! The hit-and-run driver was not arrested. But where did this happen? Who was there to know it was a hit-and-run driver. Someone must have been watching to see it happen, but who was this 3rd eye? Why was his funeral rushed? They didn't even wait for his wife to see his remains before burial. Why the rush? They didn't want them to see that he was shot and not knocked down by a car. Just as Archibong was killed and arranged like an accident. While the killings go on, the military government of Babangida opened the way for Advanced Fee Fraud. He started the Finance Houses; fraudsters to swindle used this. Forum Group was one, Ade Bendel, Fred Ajudua, late Maurice Ibekwe and others.

In 1987, Chief Obafemi Awolowo died. It was a shock to Nigerians, not because the death was untimely, not because he died at a tender age, but we were not expecting that the man would die so soon even at his age. He was seen dead on the floor in his bathroom. What could kill Baba Awolowo? They said cardiac arrest. Is this true? The rumour then was that Pa Awolowo committed suicide after he was confronted by IBB on some findings. Let us say this is true, (which can never be anyway), what could have been the issue that Chief Awolowo would have to take his life for? The life he did not take during the treasonable felony trial. If he did not commit suicide, what killed him? It is known that one of his last visits was to Dodan Barracks; the landlord of Dodan Barracks that is IBB entertained him. Did he drink tea like MKO Abiola?

During the coup that brought in Buhari, one thing that was not clear to Buhari and others was that there was another coup within their own coup. The position of the Chief of Army Staff was for Bako, the man who was to deliver Shagari, but Babangida was also interested in that same position. He knew why he wanted it. It was to position himself for eventual take over from Buhari. All the General Officers Commanding report to the Chief of Army Staff which was the chain of command before 1985. They do not report to the Head of state or President directly, and to succeed in any coup, you need these GOCs, since they are in direct contact with the soldiers and whatever may be needed for the coup, in terms of troops, weapons and ammunitions. To displace Bako, a plan was hatched to bring someone in to coordinate the coup in Abuja, the man now a Senator was recalled from Harare where he was serving, though he was to coordinate the coup in Abuja, his actual mission was to stop Bako. Eventually Bako died in the coup allegedly shot from the back. But no one ever queried that. That he was shot from the back showed clearly that he did not die during gun battle but was killed. It was a case of a coup within a coup.

In mid-October, 1991, General Babangida cut short his visit to the Commonwealth Heads of Government Conference in Zimbabwe when violence broke out in Kano. Hundreds were killed in several days of violence following the announcement of an open-air Christian revival.

According to Christian refugees, security forces did not act decisively at the outset because of fears of provoking the Islamic leadership in the area. When violence escalated, the police fired indiscriminately at crowds, using live ammunition.

Ibrahim Babangida was among the junior officers who joined hands in the killing of innocent Biafrans during the civil war. Though he later married the late Maryam who dies of cancer recently, she was from Asaba, the very location where people were made to face a big pit and then shot from back. People fell into that pit and were buried in mass graves. Those people were killed to avenge the death of Sarduana of Sokoto in the hands of the Major Chukwuma Kaduna Nzeogwu led revolutionaries. Genocide took place in Asaba and is well documented just like other parts of Biafra.

It is Babangida's policy position that is causing deaths in the Niger Delta. People he put in positions of authority are behind the killings of the indigenous land owners who are being killed by the army and police to enable Nigeria harvest the oil fields.

CHAPTER FIVE

But no nation can base its survival and development on luck and prayers alone while its leadership fritters away every available opportunity for success and concrete achievement. **Ibrahim Babangida**

IBB and his ill gotten wealth

What he lacks in public acceptance, Babangida abundantly possesses in wealth and exotic living outside office. The former Military President has a hilltop mansion in Minna where he receives visitors from within and outside the country as early as 6am. He had hosted society's high and mighty to many eye-popping social parties, like the marriage ceremonies of his children, at the mansion. He is widely believed to have owned among others, Heritage Press in Abuja, publisher of the defunct Crystal Magazines. The former President Olusegun Obasanjo was said to have denied license for the establishment of Heritage University as a private university. His late wife Maryam, owned the popular El-Amin International School, which consists of Playgroup, Nursery, Primary and Secondary Schools with plan on to set up the El-Amin University. Mrs. Babangida also owns El-Amin Bakery and Confectionery, makers of one of the most expensive bread in the country.

In the area of managing the national economy, Babangida bestowed his adroitness and moral degeneracy. His economy was dominated by male-wives, particularly in the banking and oil sectors. Women often brag about the efficacy of 'bottom' power. Feminine men sometimes flaunt it too as their passport to economic liberation. Between them and the suddenly very lucrative 419 business of the time, industry was complete. IBB's chiefs, allegedly colluded with 419 criminals to create the over-night semi-illiterate money-bags without class or shame, (including the 150 members of the National Assembly, that in 2005 sent IBB a birthday card), and who together now form the bulk of his supporters and campaigners, to return him to power.

Babangida (sapped) or totally wiped the middle class out of existence with the destruction of the naira, which he did by fiat in 1985, when he down graded the naira exchange rate from about N2 to N18 to the dollar. By the time he was forced out of office in 1993, the naira was exchanging at N60 to the dollar. Society was now reduced to two social classes of either the very poor or the rich rogues.

There is this strong allegation among the rank and file of the armed forces, and members of the defense correspondence of our newspapers attached to the seat of power, that Babangida arranged, in the last couple of weeks before leaving office, several armoured vehicle loads of newly printed naira notes to be delivered daily to his new Minna palatial abode obviously with the connivance of Abacha, perhaps as his mentor's retirement benefit. Abacha and Babangida had several serious financial problems with Abiola but one of them takes the cake. It was over some foreign war booty amounting to US$215m. It is alleged that Babangida had asked Abiola to help launder it when Babangida was in office but Abiola was not interested.

Babangida allegedly side-stepped Abiola and eventually prevailed upon a member of Abiola's family in the custom of family friendship, to rescue the situation. Then the person suddenly died. It is further alleged that Abiola was asked to return the money and he truthfully and honestly said he knew noting about it and even if there was such a thing, he had no authority over the matter. Then he was asked to pressurize the children of the deceased to play ball. Abiola refused, arguing that he had no legal or moral right to do so. The kids of the deceased wanted Abiola released but Abiola was too principled to succumb to blackmail so the powers that be decided early after his arrest, that he would die in detention for declaring himself president.

The Gulf war oil windfall is Babangida's often-referenced loot. Abacha set up a panel headed by the highly respected economist, Pius Okigbo, in October, 1994, to reorganize the CBN. Okigbo's panel discovered that $12.2 billion of the $12.4 billion accruable from the Gulf War excess crude oil sales was frittered away or unaccounted for, through nebulous or phantom projects that could not be traced. Only $206 million was left in the account. According to Okigbo, "**disbursements were clandestinely undertaken while the country was openly reeling with crushing external debt overhead. These represent, no matter the initial justification for creating the account, a gross abuse of public trust.** "

When Obasanjo in 2001, decided to look quietly into the missing NNPC's US$12.2 billion Gulf war oil windfall linked to Babangida, it was found that the documents pertaining to the fraud had disappeared from the volts of the Central Bank. The brilliant, highly respected economist, Pius Okigbo who handled the investigations into the scam had private copies. Before he could deliver the copies, he insisted on travelling to London against strong, wise, private, counsel, and he was wasted. Other members of the Okigbo panel had copies of the report anyway and were still alive.

Government miraculously found the CBN documents when it suited it, and aspects of the documents concerning IBB, were published during the threat by members of the House of Representatives to impeach President Obasanjo in July, 2005, because of speculations that IBB was one of the Northern elite fanning the plot.

Babangida was ruthless in the way he amassed his colossal wealth. First is the illegal self-allocation of free oil, sold on the spot market. Then he initiated the corrupt culture of maintaining a huge monthly security vote virtually as personal pocket money. Rather than repair our refineries, let alone to work at maximum capacity, IBB built private refineries in Cote d'Ivoire and the Republic of Benin, where he took our crude to refine and sell back to us as fuel.

John Fashanu, in a private investigation published in African Confidential early in Obasanjo's current regime, discovered an alleged $6 billion debt buy-back scam by IBB between 1988 and 1993. Another $14.4 billion disappeared into off shore accounts as currency stabilization and debt buy-back scheme that actually cost $2.5 billion. One of the front-companies used, Growth Management, based in London, bought the debt for 10 cents per dollar and resold to the government at 45 cents to steal 35 cents per dollar. Fashanu was trying to recover about $17 billion for the Nigerian government only for the CBN to say they had no records of the deals. The records are out there abroad but cleaned out at home to conceal the (theft) deals.

The Wolfsberg Principles, an initiative of 11 banks and institutions across the world to fight serious international financial crimes, traced another $3 billion of our stolen money to Babangida's accounts abroad, and $4.3 billion to Abacha's. Although Babangida used mostly fictitious names for his numerous accounts abroad, EFCC could zero in on some of the accounts by following up on the dusts raised early in 2003 over the financing of a leading Nigerian telecommunications project in which Babangida is alleged to own 75% shares. Mohammed fronts for his father on the authentic board of the company. Those claiming to have borrowed from foreign banks in the heat of the EFCC's revelations at the time have not identified the collateral or sortie used. Documents on the loan supposed to have been granted on 9 February, 2001, was dated 28 August, 2006. The original 'loan' letter has not been presented. Apparently, Paribas Bank, based in Paris, was managing a slush fund from which investments in excess of US$400 million was made to buy into Alcatel, (the telecommunications' partner technical partners), Bouygues Telecoms, Peugeot and Total finaelf.

Alcatel and Parabel National of France were worried at the time that their invoices for the telecom project were being inflated to launder funds by the supposed private owners of the sources of funds and that private cheques were being issued to finance the staggering project without recourse to borrowing from banks. They suspected illegal laundering of funds and threatened to withdraw collaboration on the project while alerting Interpol to investigate the sources of the private cheques being issued to finance the project.

IBB could not participate in Obasanjo's 2003, inauguration ceremonies, because he was allegedly out of the country sorting out the Interpol queries on the Alcatel's slush account alert, at the time. Even now, the telecoms' financing details through Siemens etc could be investigated by the EFCC tracing ghost cheques to issuing private sources of funds and their local and international banks to unravel possible laundering of funds.

Luscious contracts for the construction of Abuja were awarded to front-companies of his and his cronies, including Julius Berger and Arab Contractors that between them virtually single-handedly handled the construction of the new Federal Capital. The security danger of foreign companies solely constructing a country's capital and having assess to its structural secrets, including possible Presidential underground escape routes and military arsenal volts, is mind boggling to say the least, but that is an issue for another day.

The largest, most prestigious housing estate in Alexandra, Egypt's leading holiday resort town is alleged to belong to Babangida. Even Egyptians cannot afford his rent, which is alleged to be in dollars. All his tenants are rich foreigners and the staff of multi-national companies operating in Alexandra. The estate is alleged to have its own airport, which Babangida uses when he visits.

Babangida is alleged to own several other housing estates around the world, including houses on Bishop Avenue in London. He uses his London houses; it is alleged, as guest houses or gifts for people on his compromise list. He is considered generous with gifts of cars with their boots stuffed with naira notes when he wants some jobs done.

Almost all the principal characters involved in leadership tussles with Babangida since 1985, Abiola, Yar Adua, Idiagbon and even Abacha, have all died through induced cardiac arrest, lethal injection, poisoned food, gassed telephone handset, etc and my fear is whether Nigeria would survive the Godfather himself?

Bank of Credit and Commerce International
The Bank of Credit and Commerce International (BCCI) was a major international bank founded in 1972 by Agha Hasan Abedi, a Pakistani financier. The Bank was registered in Luxembourg. Within a decade BCCI touched its peak. It operated in 78 countries, had over 400 branches, and had assets in excess of US$20 billion, making it the 7th largest private bank in the world by assets.

In the late 1980's BCCI became the target of a two-year undercover operation conducted by the US Customs Service. This operation concluded with a fake wedding that was attended by BCCI officers and drug dealers from around the world who had established a personal friendship and working relationship with undercover Special Agent Robert Mazur. After a six month trial in Tampa, key bank officers were convicted and received lengthy prison sentences. Bank officers began cooperating with law enforcement authorities and that cooperation caused BCCI's many crimes to be revealed.

BCCI came under the scrutiny of regulatory bodies and intelligence agencies in the 1980s due to its perceived avoidance of falling under one regulatory banking authority, a fact that was later, after extensive investigations, proven to be false. BCCI became the focus of a massive regulatory battle in 1991 and was described as a "$20-billion-plus heist".

Investigators in the U.S. and the UK revealed that BCCI had been "set up deliberately to avoid centralized regulatory review, and operated extensively in bank secrecy jurisdictions. Its affairs were extraordinarily complex. Its officers were sophisticated international bankers whose apparent objective was to keep their affairs secret, to commit fraud on a massive scale, and to avoid detection."

The liquidators, Deloitte & Touche, filed a lawsuit against Price Waterhouse and Ernst & Young - the bank's auditors - which was settled for $175 million in 1998. A further lawsuit against the Emir of Abu Dhabi, a major shareholder, was launched in 1999 for approximately $400 million. BCCI creditors also instituted a $1 billion suit against the Bank of England as a regulatory body. After a nine-year struggle, due to the Bank's statutory immunity, the case went to trial in January 2004. However, in November 2005, Deloitte convinced creditor Abu Dhabi to drop its claims against the Bank of England, except for a claim for return of its deposits, in that Abu Dhabi owned 77% of the bank shares at closing, and was therefore also facing a major lawsuit. To date liquidators have recovered about 75% of the creditors' lost money.

The BCCI Affairs in the world.
A Report to the Committee on Foreign Relations
United States Senate
by
Senator John Kerry and Senator Hank Brown
December 1992
102d Congress 2d Session Senate Print 102-140

In his July 29, 1992 indictment of BCCI's former heads, Agha Hasan Abedi and Swaleh Naqvi, and two of BCCI's front-men, Ghaith Pharaon and Faisal Saud Al Fulaij, New York District Attorney Robert Morgenthau alleged, in some detail, how BCCI systematically engaged in criminal activity with officials and prominent political figures from many countries to generate assets for BCCI's Ponzi scheme, both from the governments involved, and from innocent, legitimate depositors.

As the indictment alleges:

. . . members of the BCC Group, acting to further the conduct and affairs of the criminal enterprise, assisted various nations, including Pakistan, Senegal, Zambia and Nigeria, to evade fiscal restraints placed on them by such world institutions as the World Bank and the International Monetary Fund. . . . The BCC Group agreed to bribe employees, agents and fiduciaries entrusted with Third World money to place it at risk in the BCC Group, which was insolvent.

Members of the enterprise sought to secure a preferential position for the BCC Group in various countries through the use of corrupt payments of monies and other benefits to powerful individuals and to make and cause to be made deposits of money with the BCC Group. Specifically, defendants Abedi and Naqvi plotted to deliver cash and other benefits to countries' finance ministers, head of countries' central banks and senior executives of international and regional organizations to obtain deposits. . .

Among the countries in which members of the BCC group made such corrupt payments for deposits and favorable treatment were the Congo, **Nigeria**, Morocco, Senegal, Tunisia, the Ivory Coast, Argentina and Peru. Among the institutions defrauded were the World Bank, the International

Monetary Fund, the African Development Bank and the Economic Cooperation of West African States

Similarly, over the past four years, the Subcommittee has developed extensive documentary and testimonial evidence of BCCI's systematic reliance on relationships with, and as necessary, payments to, prominent political figures in most of the 73 countries in which BCCI operated. BCCI records and testimony from former BCCI officials together document BCCI's systematic securing of Central Bank deposits of Third World countries; its provision of favors to political figures; and its reliance on those figures to provide BCCI itself with favors in times of need.

As BCCI's former senior official for the Caribbean, Abdur Sakhia, testified:

BCCI's strategy globally had been to be very well-known, to make an impact in the marketplace, to have contacts or relationships . . . with all the people who matter. . . You name it, we would develop relationships with everyone of consequence . . . In the Caribbean, every major country I knew the heads of state, I knew the finance ministers, I knew the governors of the central bank. I knew heads of all the major banks in the area, the heads of foreign banks. I knew the people in various official agencies, like the Caribbean Development Bank, Inter-American Development Bank, Organization of American States. Everyone of consequence in this region I knew. . . .

These relationships were systematically turned to BCCI's use to generate cash needed to prop up its books. BCCI would obtain an important figure's agreement to give BCCI deposits from a country's Central Bank, exclusive handling of a country's use of U.S. commodity credits, preferential treatment on the processing of money coming in and out of the country where monetary controls were in place, the right to own a bank, secretly if necessary, in countries where foreign banks were not legal, or other questionable means of securing assets or profits. In return, BCCI would pay bribes to the figure, or otherwise give him other things he wanted in a simple quid-pro-quo. For example, BCCI would help an official move flight capital out of his country to a safe haven elsewhere, to launder funds skimmed by the official from an official bank account or official commercial transaction, create a foundation for a head of state to provide charitable services for his home village or province, take him on a shopping spree at a fancy London department store, or secure him sexual favors.

The result was that BCCI had relationships that ranged from the questionable, to the improper, to the fully corrupt with officials from countries all over the world, including but certainly not limited to Argentina, Bangladesh, Botswana, Brazil, Cameroon, China, Colombia, the Congo, Ghana, Guatemala, the Ivory Coast, India, Jamaica, Kuwait, Lebanon, Mauritius, Morocco, **Nigeri**a, Pakistan, Panama, Peru, Saudi Arabia, Senegal, Sri Lanka, Sudan, Suriname, Tunisia, the United Arab Emirates, the United Kingdom, the United States, Zambia, and Zimbabwe.
The result was that BCCI had relationships that ranged from the questionable, to the improper, to the fully corrupt with officials from countries all over

the world, including but certainly not limited to Argentina, Bangladesh, Botswana, Brazil, Cameroon, China, Colombia, the Congo, Ghana, Guatemala, the Ivory Coast, India, Jamaica, Kuwait, Lebanon, Mauritius, Morocco, Nigeria, Pakistan, Panama, Peru, Saudi Arabia, Senegal, Sri Lanka, Sudan, Suriname, Tunisia, the United Arab Emirates, the United Kingdom, the United States, Zambia, and Zimbabwe.

Typically, these relationships were handled personally and in secrecy by BCCI's top two officials -- Abedi and Naqvi -- with the occasional assistance of trusted lieutenants. Accordingly, a full accounting of these relationships may not be possible. Sakhia told the Subcommittee that he believed there was a list of BCCI's payments to political figures somewhere at BCCI's headquarters in London, held closely by Abedi and Naqvi that contained all the names. When BCCI's headquarters were moved to Abu Dhabi in the spring of 1990, the list, if it still existed, was likely moved there with BCCI's other records:

There was a world wide list of people who were in the payoff of BCCI. The family of Indira Gandhi, President [Ershad] of Bangladesh, General Zia of Pakistan. Many of the leaders of Africa. I went to a World Bank meeting in Seoul, Korea and [BCCI official] Alauddin Shaikh was handing out cash in the hall to the staff of the **Central Bank of Nigeria** . . . Abedi's philosophy was to appeal to every sector. If you were religious people he would help you pray. President Carter's main thing was charity, so he gave Carter charity. [Pakistani] President Zia's brother-in-law needed a job, he got a job. [Bangladeshi] President [Ershad]'s mistress needed a job, she got a job. You needed the admission of your son to a top college? Abedi would arrange it somehow.

According to Sakhia, the form of the payoff varied with the needs of the customers, but the purpose was always the same -- "to buy influence."

Deposits from Foreign Governments

A baseline for assessing BCCI's principal relationships with foreign governments is to review the deposits it received from Central Banks. At one level, the choice of BCCI as a depository for a Central Bank of a Third World country might seem logical. BCCI had marketed itself as the Third World bank, devoted to providing the best possible services to the Third World. However, every central banker also knew that BCCI, as a bank not based in any one country, had no lender of last resort, and no consolidated audit.

Thus, deposits in BCCI were potentially a very substantial risk for any Central Bank. If BCCI failed, the Central Bank funds would not be protected, but would be treated like the funds of any other depositor. Despite these obvious risks to placing funds with BCCI, dozens of countries placed their reserves with the bank, in some cases, at very substantial, and imprudent, levels.

Loans to Foreign Governments and Government Banks

As a consequence of BCCI's collapse, determining what governments were credited by BCCI as receiving loans is a far easier matter than determining who, in the past, placed funds with BCCI. A consolidated loan report for BCCI dating from March 31, 1991, shows numerous governmental organizations credited as receiving very substantial lending from BCCI as follows:

Abu Dhabi Finance Department	$35,704,000
Abu Dhabi National Food Stuff Co.	21,749,000
Banca Nazional Del Lavaro	13,737,000
Botswana Railways	9,400,000
Botswana Telecommunications	2,600,000
Cameroon Ministry of Finance	29,172,000
China International Water & Elec	42,268,000
China National Complete Plant Exp	32,606,000
China Road & Bridge Eng. Co.	20,641,000
China State Construction Group	32,450,000
State of Gabon	7,771,000
Bank of Jamaica	33,895,000
Central Bank of Nigeria	**226,060,000**
Sultanate of Oman	14,444,000
Petrojam (Jamaica Petroleum)	45,420,000
Government of Seychelles	22,957,000
Bank of Sudan	53,987,000
Republic of Zimbabwe	17,063,000

Price Waterhouse reports 18 months earlier had listed BCCI's exposure on lending to governments and Central Banks as follows:

Country	Nature of	Exposure 9/30/89 (in millions)
Nigeria	Government	216.9
Philippines	Central Bank	30
Zambia	Central Bank	24.6
Sudan	Central Bank	19.9
Iraq	Unspecified	11.8
Mexico	Unspecified	7.3
Cuba	Unspecified	2.3
Sierra Leone	Unspecified	3.3
Ivory Coast	Unspecified	.8
Panama	Unspecified	.6

Many normal banks have such exposures, and apart from the situation involving Nigeria and to some extent Sudan, the exposure faced by BCCI on its lending to governments was within reasonable commercial norms. However, beneath the veneer of normal practice, the underlying manner by which BCCI developed these relationships was anything but normal. As the case histories below demonstrate, in country after country, BCCI's relationships with officials were fundamentally corrupt.

Using a nominee was a typical way of going about things. Argentina, Brazil, Ghana, Colombia, Venezuela, **Nigeria**. All these places started out as nominee relationships. Some were cleaned up. But it was always preferable that there not be a nominee relationship. When we bought a bank or set up a subsidiary, we would often use the nominee relationship because the laws of the country wouldn't allow BCC to have majority control. For example, we used it briefly in Colombia until we received permission to have majority control for BCCI from the government. (13)

In each case, various forms of payments for the individuals who facilitated the purchases of the banks were made by BCCI, including bribes to officials in many of the countries.

Money Laundering, Commodities Frauds and Skimming

According to BCCI officers interviewed by the Subcommittee, there were consistent themes in BCCI's activities in the Third World, in terms of the kinds of services that government officials would be looking for from BCCI. First, to the extent the official controlled a source of government funds, the official typically wanted to be compensated in connection with his decision on where to place the funds. The solution to this problem was simple enough -- BCCI would pay a "commission" to the official involved. Second, to the extent the official controlled transactions involving government funds, the official might well want to be compensated on a fee basis, transaction by transaction. BCCI developed a number of techniques in response to this requirement, which typically involved one form or another of skimming the government funds that moved through the transaction, again with the revenues deposited in a safe place outside the official's country. Third, to the extent the official was in a position to generate substantial resources of his own through non-BCCI corruption, he often would want a safe and confidential place to hide his money. Again, BCCI would comply.

In each of these cases, BCCI would make use of applicable techniques for hiding and laundering cash: manager's ledgers or numbered accounts; phony loans to hide (and legitimize) real, but unclean deposits; circuitous routing of funds through bank secrecy havens like the Grand Caymans and Panama, and so on.

Pay-Offs to Avoid Prosecution

Inevitably, BCCI's criminal practices as a bank would set off alarm bells in one or another of the nations in which it was operating. Because of BCCI's underlying financial fragility, any such problem could potentially mushroom. Accordingly, the bank made it a high priority to fix such cases through payoffs. Usually, this could be accomplished with existing relationships.

For example, in Nigeria, on the several occasions when BCCI's activities had been discovered by officials who had not been compromised, investigations were quelled by a top Nigerian religious and governmental official, Al Haji Ibrahim Dasuki, who was also president of BCCI's Nigerian bank.

References
- *A Conflict of Interest: 'Fraud and the Collapse of Titans'* *Bartholomew B. J. Henderson*

- *Robert Mazur:"The Infiltrator: My Secret Life Inside the Dirty Banks Behind Pablo Escobar's Medellin Cartel", Little, Brown & Co.,NY,2009, ISBN 978-0-316-07753-8*
- *J. Beaty, S.C. Gwynne: The Outlaw Bank: A Wild Ride into the Secret Heart of BCCI. Random House, 1993, ISBN 0-679-41384-7.*
- *"The BCCI Affair", Report to the Committee on Foreign Relations, United States Senate, Senator John Kerry and Senator Hank Brown, 1992, 102nd Congress 2nd Session Senate Print 102-140 (Kerry Report).*
- *Time Magazine, 29.July 1991, The world's sleaziest bank, online unter Cover Story: The Dirtiest Bank of All*
- *Tell Magazine of July 24, 1995*

THE FULL OPERATION OF BCCI IN NIGERIA...

BCCI's activities in Nigeria were so profoundly; overwhelmingly corrupt as to suggest a very significant level of corruption in Nigerian officialdom generally. Whereas BCCI's activities in most countries merely involved corrupting a few key people, in Nigeria the corruption was systemic and endemic, and touched nearly every operation of the bank in country.

According to BCCI officers, this was not the consequence of BCCI applying its practices to Nigeria, but rather, BCCI adapting itself to the conditions already present in Nigeria. According to BCCI officers interviewed by the Subcommittee, few European or American businesses active in Nigeria would have been able to do business without making one or another form of pay-off to Nigerian officials during the 1980's, and, to the knowledge of some BCCI officials, several such corporations, including some well-known European and U.S. banks, did.

During the Subcommittee's original investigation of BCCI in 1988, corruption involving Nigerian officials was one of the earliest allegations of BCCI criminality made to staff. As former Subcommittee investigator Jack Blum testified:

There are extraordinarily close relationships at all levels of the Nigerian Government with BCCI. [During the intial investigation of the source] he had been called . . . by the Nigerian Ambassador who had been asked by the President [of Nigeria] to say, what's happening here? What are you guys doing with respect to BCCI?

Several BCCI officials described BCCI having made cash payments to officials of the Nigerian central bank. As Abdur Sakhia testified:

During a meeting of the World Bank in Seoul, Korea -- he think it was in 1985 -- he saw one of the BCC officers with a lot of cash, handing it out to the staff of the central bank of Nigeria. This is what he saw personally being given to them.

The most detailed account of BCCI's activities in Nigeria came from Nazir Chinoy, convicted in the Tampa case of money laundering during the time he was BCCI's Francophone regional manager. Prior to moving to BCCI-Paris, Chinoy had been stationed by BCCI in Nigeria for the first half of the 1980's, where he saw first hand the pervasive corruption of the Nigerian banking system, and BCCI's solutions for dealing with it profitably.

At the time Chinoy arrived in Nigeria in December, 1980, he found that BCCI already had purchased a minority interest in a commercial bank in Nigeria -- owning just 40 percent of the Nigerian bank, with corrupt Nigerian officials insisting on controlling the remaining 60 percent. But even with only 40 percent, the Nigerian offices of BCCI were earning BCCI very significant profits. In fact, the profits were so large that BCCI feared the Nigerians might try to take remaining interest in the bank away from BCCI. Chinoy's job was to establish a second bank for BCCI in Nigeria to protect BCCI against the possible expropriation by the government of the first bank.

BCCI was already being used for short-term commercial financing through letters of credit for the purchase and sale of goods by various Nigerian governmental entities. Moreover, some Nigerian officials were using BCCI in London and elsewhere to store cash they had earned through off-the-books deals while in the government. As Chinoy explained:

Nigerians were keeping large laundered funds generated by influential people who got contracts from international companies and commissions paid abroad. The money was kept abroad and not repatriated to Nigeria. BCCI was a good place to keep it. The simplest means of generating funds for Nigerian officials was requiring a "commission" on each transaction. As Chinoy stated:

Commission means kick-back. The government approves a $300 million contract. A multinational corporation agrees with the government which has helped him, 10 percent gets kicked back. A company is established abroad or they nominate a cousin or someone who is paid 3 percent. It is known as a commission but it is actually a kickback.

Other mechanisms by which these funds were generated for Nigerian officials were through over invoicing of imports and under invoicing of exports. When over invoicing would take place, the government would pay more for goods than the actual market price. BCCI would disguise this through shell entities which would appear to any outsider as arms-length brokers, but which in fact were mere mechanisms by which money would be skimmed off from the government and deposited in BCCI, to be shared by BCCI and by the official responsible for handling the purchase. When under invoicing would take place, the reverse would happen. The government would ship greater commodities than were reflected on the government invoices; the additional commodity would be sold at the same time as that invoiced, and the additional funds generated would again be split by BCCI and the Nigerian official, who of course would have keep his profits outside his home country. As Chinoy explained it:

Essentially, BCCI was handling the financing of commodities through bribery. For example, BCCI loaned $250 million to Nigeria to be repaid within the next six months for oil exports. Nigeria would charge OPIC prices but would load ten percent more than the invoice. That way you are giving a 10 percent discount. Business was so good that Chinoy's predecessor and superior at BCCI, Alauddin Shaikh, who was a senior official at the bank, decided to leave BCCI to form a partnership with a Nigerian, Razar Sareef, who had gained control of Nigerian oil exports. Shaikh has been implicated by numerous BCCI officials in making pay-offs not only in Nigeria, but in several other countries. His new venture was in any case a success. It wound up controlling the National Petroleum Corporation of Nigeria account for the United States, an account it continued to control at least as of 1991.

Other techniques used by Nigerian officials with the connivance of BCCI were currency swaps involving government funds. Government funds were placed in an account at BCCI in London. BCCI would place the funds with Lloyds or another bank and swap it into different currencies or make stock investments with it. If there was a loss, Nigeria bore it. If there was a profit, the first 8 percent went to Nigeria, on anything additional, the money was split between Nigeria and the traders at BCCI.

In addition to the skimming that was taking place of government funds, BCCI found itself in the position of being able to earn enormous fees from ordinary commercial transactions in Nigeria, because Nigerian officials insured that financial transactions undertaken by BCCI for its customers would be handled much more efficiently than similar transactions undertaken by any other foreign bank doing business in Nigeria. While other banks would have to wait days or weeks for their transactions to be processed by the relevant government ministries, BCCI, would have their transactions handled promptly. As Chinoy explained:

BCCI got big profits because early release of foreign exchange was the crux of any deal. BCCI was two to three times faster than Chase Manhattan or the Bank of America or any other joint venture. BCCI was faster than any Nigerian bank in getting foreign exchange out of the Central Bank. It had very good relations with Central Bank of Nigeria. Unless you were friendly with receptionist, it would lie in the tray and wouldn't go anywhere for days. BCCI used to look after the girl at the foreign exchange desk. When the BCCI clerk would hand in the foreign exchange she would do that first for processing its release.

Release of foreign exchange was important. Clerks at every level were looked after by presents. We had an officer, Mr. Saddiqui, who used to go and spend at least 10 days a month in Nigeria. His specific job was to look after people at all levels. In addition, he had appointed one to two expatriates who did nothing but spend their time at Central Bank. I do not think that cash was actually paid, but presents were bought in large amounts, as much as 20-40 dresses, shirts, ties at a time brought in from London and given. Everybody was kept happy. So that there is no objection raised by a clerk that a document isn't filled in exactly correctly. Because BCCI was so good and there was a BCCI application where someone had forgot to cross a "t" or dot an "i" and they would get it rectified quickly. This is Nigeria.

The result was that BCCI began to develop almost a monopoly on handling import-export financing in Nigeria. As Chinoy explained: For banks other than BCCI, sometimes it could take 90 days for your letter of credit to take. If some clerk is unhappy he says your documents are not in order and he throws it back and doesn't give a reason. In Nigeria it is very important to have contacts because it takes 14 days for a letter to reach you. BCCI would get its letters of credit three times faster than anyone else. They will get it through the Central Bank faster than other banks. Business increases due to this reputation.

According to Chinoy, the price-tag on some of the presents provided Nigerian bureaucrats was not small -- typically, they included such items as silver canteens, cutlery sets, tea sets, coffee sets, and $5,000 luxury watches and similar goods valued at a few thousand pounds, and given to Central Bank and other Nigerian officials.

Chinoy knew about the corruption of top Nigerian officials personally. During his residence in Nigeria, three Nigerians controlled the release of foreign exchange in Nigeria. One of the three, the country's comptroller of foreign exchange, was named Al Haji Balu:

Once when the source of this information was in marketing in 1985-1986, he saw a deposit from Balu of 280,000 Deutschmarks in a certificate of deposit in Frankfort. He knew what his salary in Nigeria was. This was at the time worth about $150,000 US, for deposit at BCCI Frankfort. He didn't have that kind of money from his government salary. It was obvious what was going on.

Another extremely prominent Nigerian political figure who was being paid bribes by BCCI was Al Haji Ibrahim Dasuki, chairman of BCC Nigeria up until 1990-1991, when he became the Sultan of Sokoto. BCCI audit records show a $1 million loan from BCCI to Dasuki which BCCI provided him to pay for his shares of BCCI-Nigeria. Dasuki repaid this favor -- although not this loan -- to BCCI in many ways. According to Chinoy:

Dasuki had fantastic contacts with the government. He was a politician and religious leader of great eminence and in line then to be Sultan of Sokoto. He could help the bank and used to be paid. He was paid from Caymans as well as from Nigeria. He was paid in London by one of Mr. Naqvi's special assistants, Asad Matualah, now in custody in Abu Dhabi.

Chinoy explained that Dasuki was the one who would fix problems with other government officials for BCCI if anyone noticed that exchange laws were being broken or other problems arose. Dasuki was able to perform this role because of his position as a religious leader, making his support indispensable to other key Nigerian officials:

Dasuki came from the North where all presidents in Nigeria come from, and even the President has to go and pay homage to the Sultan of Sokoto. When he became Sultan all of the leaders would owe him a measure of deference. He took full advantage of that. Two to three times BCCI got into trouble and Dasuki would sort it out.

Dasuki also acted as a local representative for BCCI, obtaining the right to import goods for Nigeria, and providing that right to a business associate affiliated with BCCI. The BCCI associate would then arrange for import of the commodity involved, such as rice. According to Chinoy: It was like a license to make money. Rice was gold. Dummy companies were created on a per transaction basis and had no other life beyond that.

Dasuki had so much business activity, he was able to establish his nephew, Ibrahim Katuni, to a level where by the mid-1980's, every foreign country did business with him because he had access to every ministry and had cut deals with each of them. Katuni would tell a foreign businessman, this is how you'll make $100,000, and I'll take 20 percent. He kept Dasuki happy and was hoping to become President of BCCI.

BCCI found other ways of circumventing practices in Nigeria which frustrated other banks and prevented them functioning normally. As the indictment of BCCI officials in New York described it, BCCI's success in this area involved defrauding the Central Bank of Nigeria. Foreign exchange shortfalls in Nigeria had caused the government in about 1981 to impose restrictions on imports, requiring letters of credit used in connection with imports to be secured by 100 percent cash deposits in Nigerian banks. In turn, the banks were required to certify that the payment had been made to the Central Bank. As the transactions involved might take months to be completed, this would tie up the company's funds for substantial amounts of time, discouraging the import activity altogether. BCCI's way around the problem was to create phony loans for the importers and deposit the "proceeds" from the phony loans on BCCI's books in Nigeria, and then inform the Central Bank that the deposits had been made. Once the import transaction was over, the paperwork would be reversed. Through this technique, BCCI generated letter-of-credit business from importers who would not otherwise have been able to do business; earned commissions on opening the letters of credit; earned interest on the fictitious loans it granted; and realized exchange profits from converting currencies.

BCCI also handled black market foreign exchange transactions for Nigerian officials for use in Nigerian elections. Because Nigeria has never developed credit cards, and Nigerians rarely use checks, essentially all transactions in Nigeria are in cash, with few record-keeping requirements adequate to monitor graft, which is endemic. Most of the time, officials sell their cash in Nigerian currency and buy foreign exchange with it for purchasing goods abroad, or for maintaining deposits and homes abroad, typically in the United Kingdom. But sometimes the Nigerians found they needed Nigerian currency, especially during election time. According to Chinoy: At elections, the officials need the money and sell the foreign exchange at black market price and that money is paid in Nigerian currency to them and they return the foreign exchange abroad. This method is employed by Nigerian politicians to obtain political money. It is commonplace throughout Africa.

As noted above, BCCI's Nigerian operations were among the bank's most profitable. This is understandable. In the case of BCCI and the Nigerian government, crime paid.
Babangida once noted that, "the work of Nigeria is not complete for as long as there is any one Nigerian who goes to bed on empty stomach" but his policy left millions in poverty.

Babangida usurped eight years and eight months of the thirty-three years of military misrule and still wants to come back to finish us off properly. If he was honest with himself, he ought to be ashamed for the economic, political and social mess he has turned Nigeria into. Babangida should be heading for Kirikiri not Aso Rock.

IBB and Vasta's death?

There are many other thousands of innocent people in the grave whom IBB murdered. Their souls are crying for justice. All those he made widows and orphans are seeking justice. He has no hiding place. Should anybody or group of persons make any mago mago to force IBB on Nigerians, the Aba women riot of 1929 will be a child's play to the women riot that will be witnessed in 2007(now 2011)–Vatsa's wife.

Sava Farm, a nondescript piece of property situated at Malali area of Kaduna city, does not reveal the importance of its occupant. It is owned by Hajia Sufiya, widow of General Mamman Vatsa, executed over a controversial coup by the regime of General Ibrahim Babangida in 1986. With its brown gate, half brick, half metal perimeter fence that looks as if it would collapse any time with the heavy rains, and the rusty signboard defaced by four posters of Isiah Balat who is campaigning to be governor of Kaduna State, the farm stands as a relic, in sharp contrast to the more prosperous-looking Federal Government College and the Kaduna State Water Board nearby.

Like her property, Hajia Sufiya Vatsa is a lone historical figure, abandoned in her woes and penury by successive governments after IBB executed her husband over a questionable coup. During a visit to her Sava Farm by three journalists from TheNEWS, the woman cut the picture of Miss Havisham in Charles Dickens' Great Expectations, who, after being disappointed by her suitor, refuses to see the sun, fails to change her wedding gown and leaves her watch permanently "at twenty minutes to nine." Unlike Miss Havisham, however, Sufiya's separation from her husband came from the machination of a third party – IBB. Since then, life has been horrible for her family. Daily, Sufiya sits by two high-definition photographs of her husband: one in mufti and the other in military gear.

Another symbol of her state of mind and the neglect she suffers was an abandoned grey aquarium, tilting against the wall under the portrait of a medieval soldier riding a chariot, shooting an arrow. Under another congested table in front of her was a green book, Makers of Modern Africa. A reading lamp, about four chandeliers and a dining table required dusting just as her life requires rehabilitation.

Sufiya's journey into the abyss of poverty began on 23 December 1985. The family had just concluded plans to travel to Calabar because, usually, they spent the yuletide in the Cross River State capital (Sufiya is Efik), the Id-el-Fitri in Minna, Niger State and the Id-el Kabir in Kaduna. After the necessary packing for the trip, the family waited for the return of General Vatsa from the Armed Forces Ruling Council, (AFRC), meeting he had attended. He returned home late, so the trip was postponed till the following day. At about 12 midnight, while Sufiya was watching a movie in her bedroom, her husband, who was working in his study, rushed in to tell her that IBB had sent for him. The wife protested that it was too late in the night and that Vatsa should phone his boss to shift the meeting to the following morning.

As this debate was going on, Lt. Col. U.K. Bello led a team of soldiers to Vatsa's home at Rumens Street, Ikoyi, Lagos. The soldiers, who came with armoured vehicles and military vans, surrounded the house. Vatsa told his wife who was upstairs to peep through the window. Unable to contain her fear, she rushed downstairs and insisted that if the soldiers would take away her husband, then she had to follow them. Sufiya insisted on driving Vatsa in her own Pengeot 404. At this point, Vatsa directed that the children be woken up, and he kissed them one after the other.

Haruna, the first son, who was in Military Training School, Zaria, followed them downstairs, weeping. While UK Bello drove in the fore of the convoy, Sufiya and Vatsa were chauffeur-driven in their own car in what later turned out to be a merry-go-round about Lagos till about 2 a.m when they stopped at 7 Cameron Road, Ikoyi. Vatsa was ordered out of the car. As he made to enter the building, Sufiya ran after him but she was rudely pulled back by the soldiers. The General turned and gave his wife a bear hug, an embrace that was their last. He urged his wife to take care of their children. Sufiya returned home dejected. To her shock, the military authorities had withdrawn the official domestic staff. At 5a.m, she prepared breakfast of fried yam and pawpaw, drove to her husband's detention centre but was told she could not bring in any food.

Another surprise awaited Vatsa's wife. A soldier came in and said: "Madam, Oga's wife, Mrs Mariam Babangida, said I should carry General Vatsa's telephone handset to her." Fatima, Vatsa's daughter, clung to the gadget. A struggle ensued between the 15-year-old girl and the soldier, whose muscles bulged like the biceps of Michaelangelo's statues. Sufia asked her daughter to let go of the probably bugged set.

Worse still, some gruff, fierce-looking soldiers, led by Vatsa's former Aide-de-Camp (ADC), Captain Maku, an intelligence officer of Idoma extraction, had led other soldiers in laying siege to the family's house. "Madam, no visitors, no phone calls, no going out," Maku snapped as he reclined on a settee in the living room, an improvised toothpick, peeping out of a corner of his mouth. When Sufiya protested that the family needed to buy foodstuff, Maku, whose friendly disposition when he was Vatsa's batman had changed, commanded that the woman and her children "must manage."

After three days of captivity, Sufiya could not endure it any longer. She told Maku: "Look, I am going to the market. If you refuse me, it means between you and I, somebody will die. I will show you I am a soldier's wife." She took her car, and without bothering about the soldiers, who cocked their guns menacingly at her, rammed it into the gate, which gave way as the soldiers scattered capriciously in different directions. She got to Falomo, bought bread and eggs, and decided to see one of her husband's friends, General Gado Nasko. Before the visit to Nasko, however, Sufiya had driven home and, since her daughter was, coincidentally, at the gate, had dropped the food and driven to the Naskos. Sufiya's mission was to ask Nasko to fix a meeting between her and IBB to find a way to settle the matter. Although soldiers at Nasko's house gave her the cold shoulder, her persistence worked.

Nasko, who said he was aware of the problem and would try to arrange the meeting, asked Sufiya to see him in the evening. Her hope soared. The reason was the special relationship between her family and IBB's. "When we got married," Sufiya was reported as saying, "I thought IBB and my husband were of the same family. The two wore the same size of dress and pair of shoes. IBB would drop his dirty wears in our house and put on my husband's. When IBB travelled out, for a further military training my husband took care of Mariam and her children. General Vatsa, apart from mounting the horse when IBB married Mariam, bought their first set of furniture from Leventis on hire purchase. IBB was also my husband's bestman during our wedding. Whenever Maryam's Mercedez car broke down, she used to drive my Peugeot 404. We were close." All these, to

Babangida, did not count in the field of realpolitik. Nasko told Sufiya later in the day that the military President was not ready to see her.

Another disappointment awaited Sufiya when she returned to her Rumen's Street residence, Ikoyi. A soldier from Bonny Camp was waiting for her with an order that the family should vacate the house. Another military officer said the car should be taken to Army Headquarters for security check after which they broke into the car's glove compartment and confiscated Vatsa's manuscripts. In frustration, Sufiya hired a trailer and moved the family's belongings to Kaduna. She and Fatima, however, returned and stayed in Nwakana Okoro, her brother-in-law's house at Queen's Drive, Ikoyi. When the military authorities bugged Okoro's telephone, the lawyer, a Senior Advocate, of Nigeria, became jittery.

All attempts by Sufiya to see her husband were frustrated by the military authorities. It was only Fatima's trick that worked a bit. Posing as a lawyer, she would follow other counsels into Vatsa's detention centre and trial venue. Vatsa, however, sent Sufiya a note from Kirikiri, saying: "Do not beg Babangida. He is after my life. Take care of the children. I know it is not easy but God will help you." When he was to be executed, Vatsa requested that his wrist watch and wedding ring be given to Sufiya. "But by the time they brought the watch and the wedding ring, the ring wasn't my wedding ring, so I rejected it. "Till today, they have not returned the ring to me," Sufiya was quoted by a family source.

Sufiya was, therefore, left in the cold, without any wealth to fall back on. Vatsa had only one plot of land in Abuja, but it was taken over by the late despot, General Sani Abacha. At a point, Sufiya approached General Jeremiah Useni, one-time Federal Capital Territory (FCT) Minister, in a bid to reclaim the land. Useni called for the file and told Vatsa's wife to pay for the land rent. She, however, complained to Useni: "When my husband was a minister in FCT, he refused to allocate land to me, his wife. He said it would be immoral for him to give me land. He said his successor would give me." Useni looked the other way while Sufiya and her family were deprived of the land.

Not all of Vatsa's friends abandoned the family, however. "One of his friends came to our aid." Sufiya once said. "Every other person that was dining and wining with my husband immediately switched over to IBB.

Even my children today are not identified with." To keep body, soul and the family together, Sufiya, of Efik descent, would travel to Calabar, in Cross River State, and bring food from her people to take care of her children in Kaduna where she has vowed to remain. Apart from buying and selling, Sufiya used to engage in poultry and cattle rearing. In fact, she injected life into her Sava Farm, which she set up in 1971 after the civil war. But robbers ruined the business, a situation that led to the lack of care for the premises, part of which, by the time TheNEWS visited, was overgrown with weeds.

Sufiya, therefore, has brought up her children on a shoe-string budget. Haruna, whom Vatsa asked to be withdrawn from the Nigerian Military Training School, Zaria, because of the way the Army treated him, is now married with two children. Fatima, who is studying medicine, is in London with her husband, while Jubril, who studied law, is in Minna, Niger State. Aisha is a US-based pilot.

Sufiya believes that IBB himself planned the coup. "He wrote the script, got an officer to execute." The officer in question was close to Mamma Madaki, a former military administrator of Plateau State. Apart from Major General Charles Ndiomu who once made a statement that he regretted killing Vatsa, this magazine gathered that the interview which General Domkat Bali granted TheNEWS (22 May 2006 edition) raised Sufiya's hope that justice would finally be done.

She once lamented to her husband's family: "It is painful that my husband was executed as a coup plotter even when he was not. And till this moment, we don't know where he was buried. That Gen. Domkat Bali interview published in TheNews magazine is one of the good things God has done to us in the Vatsa family. Before, some people did not believe that Vatsa was not a coup plotter; but Bali's confession explained it all. They should release the corpse of my husband to me so that he can be given a befitting burial. That is my prayer."

It was for this reason that Sufiya wrote a letter, dated 15 June 2006, to President Olusegun Obasanjo, where she stated: "Although there was no iota of evidence linking my husband with the phantom coup, he was convicted and sentenced to death by the Special Military Tribunal which purportedly tried him and other coup suspects. My husband's appeal to the

Armed Forces Ruling Council against his illegal conviction was yet to be considered when the Head of State, General Babangida had him secretly executed along with the other coup convicts."

She claimed in the letter that Bali confirmed her husband's innocence in TheNEWS' interview when he said: "'My regret is that up till now, I am not sure whether Vatsa ought to have been killed because whatever evidence they amassed against him was weak. My only regret is that I could not say, don't do it. I am not so sure whether we were right to have killed Vatsa." Sufiya, therefore, requested the Obasanjo administration to prosecute General Babangida for "the murder of my husband, General Vatsa."

Born on 3 December 1940, Major General Mamman Vatsa attended the Government Secondary School, Bida, Niger State. He enlisted in the Nigerian Army on 10 December 1962 and was trained at the Nigerian Military Training College, Kaduna and the India Military Academy.
Vatsa was in charge of the 21 Battalion during the Nigerian Civil War, after which he became an instructor at the Nigerian Defence Academy, Kaduna. Apart from his position as Principal Staff Officer at Army Headquarters, he commanded the 30 infantry Brigade (Ogoja) until July 1975. As the Commander of the Brigade of Guards, a post he held until 1979, Vatsa oversaw the movement of its headquarters from Dodan Barracks to Kofo Abayomi Street, Victoria Island, Lagos.

One proof of his loyalty to his Commander-in-Chief was when, as Commander, Brigade of Guards, Calabar, he was the first to go on air to kick against the 13 February 1976 coup, led by Lt. Col Buka Dimka. During the trial of suspects involved in that coup, he was the Tribunal Secretary. Thereafter, he was appointed the Commander, Brigade of Guards under General Olusegun Obasanjo. Mrs.Vatsa once revealed: "My husband drove General Obasanjo to his Ota farm after he handed over power to the civilians in 1979."

As Nowa Omoigui wrote, Vatsa was Commandant of the Nigerian Army School of Infantry (NASI) from 1979. "He, along with Lt. Col Bitiyong, developed the Special Warfare Wing and established the doctrinal basis for the establishment of the 82nd Composite Division of the Nigerian Army in Enugu. In fact, it was Vatsa who suggested that the Division be called the 82nd Division – after the 82nd West African Division, Burma."

As an accomplished poet and writer, Vatsa was able to publish eight poetry collections for adults and 11 for younger ones. Some of his book titles are back again at Watergate (1982), Reach For The Skies (1984), and Verses for Nigerian State Capitals (1973). His pidgin poetry collection is Tori for Geti Bow Leg (1981). His pictorial books are Bikin Suna and Stinger the Scorpion.

His literary interests transcended merely reeling out volumes of verse. He organised writing workshops for soldiers and their families, assisted the Children's Literature Association with funds, as well as allocating a piece of land in Abuja for a writers village for the Association of Nigerian Authors. Vatsa was so pre-occupied with creativity that he always carried jotters to the toilet, dining table and the bedroom. There were books strewn around in the family's apartment so much that, as TheNEWS gathered, Sufiya once threatened to "throw these books out."

Vatsa's journey to the great beyond started on 17 December 1985 when the military authorities arrested over 100 officers from the Army, Navy and the Air Force. Vatsa was picked up seven days later. They were, for two weeks, investigated by the Brigadier-General Sani Sami-led Preliminary Special Investigation Panel. After this, 17 of them were dragged before a Special Military Tribunal, set up by Bali, at the Defence Minister, at the Brigade of Guards Headquarters, Lagos. The accused officers were Lt.-Cols. Musa Bitiyong, Christian A. Oche, Micheal A Iyorshe, M. Effiong; Majors D.I Bamidele, D.E. West, J.O Onyeke and Tobias G Akwashiki. Others were Captain G.I L Sese, Lt. K.G. Dakpa, Commodore A.A. Ogwiji, Wing Commanders B.E. Ekele, Adamu Sakaba; Squadron Leaders Martin Luther, C. Ode and A Ahura.

The tribunal, chaired by Major General Ndiomu, tried the officers under the Treason and Other Offences (Special Military Tribunal) Decree 1 of 1986. Other members of the tribunal were Brigadier Yerima Yohanna Kure, Commodore Murtala Nyako, Col. Rufus Kupolati, Col E. Opaleye, and Lt. Col. D. Muhammed. Alhaji Mamman Nassarawa, a commissioner of police and Major A Kejawa, the Judge Advocate, were also members.

The IBB regime accused Vatsa of trying to overthrow it by hiding behind a farming loan to Lt-Col Bitiyong, a charge which the general denied. As Nowa Omogui, a military analyst explains in his essay, The Vatsa Conspiracy, Bitiyong was allegedly tortured to implicate Vatsa "by making reference to certain private political conversations they had, which Vatsa denied."

There were further allegations that Luther, Oche, Ogwiji and Bitiyong held a meeting at the Lagos Sheraton Hotel and Towers in November 1985. Iyorchie, Bitiyong, Oche, Ekele, Sakaba and Bamidele also allegedly met in Makurdi. Allegations such as the diversion of the presidential jet to a pre-arranged location by pilots in the executive fleet (Luther and Ahura), as Omogui put it, were floated. Oche allegedly held a meeting with Major Akwashiki, Commander of the 6th Battalion, Bonny Camp, and Onyeke, after a game of squash in Lagos and spoke about the International Monetary Fund (IMF) loan. Akwashiki was sentenced to death, but this was commuted to life imprisonment. He was however released 10 years later by the Abacha regime.

Oche, it was also alleged, mentioned the plot to his nephew, Peter Odoba, a young lieutenant of the Brigade of Guards who, as Omogui wrote, informed then Lt. Hamza al-Mustapha, an intelligence officer to the Chief of Army Staff. Obada was charged with "concealment, recommended for dismissal and a long jail term." On 6 March 1986, however, Vatsa, Iyorshe, Bamidele, Ogwiji, Ekele, Sakaba, Luther, Akura were executed.Vatsa had taken his trial and sentence with cheerful equanimity like the writer that he was. His vintage smiles revealed more than his words. "I leave you with smiles as smiles surprise people. But I will tell members of the Nigerian Army that the day you start insulting yourselves, others begin to join you," he said.

To butteress his position that there was rivalry between IBB and Vatsa, Omogui referred to an interview that Eniola Bello of THISDAY had with IBB in 2001 when he turned 60. "'Babangida said it was after Vatsa's coup was foiled that he realised his childhood friend and classmate planned the coup in line with a deep-seated personal rivalry, going back to their days as young officers. He said that unconsciously, he and Vatsa had been great competitors; that as a young officer, whatever he did Vatsa equally did and whatever Vatsa achieved, he also went after. He said it was Lt. Gen.

T.Y. Danjuma who pointed this out to him from their military records."
Babangida gave this rationalisation to justify his refusal to pardon Vatsa.
He said when he first heard his childhood friend was planning a coup, he
decided to do nothing but monitor him. He added, however, that Vatsa
came to him to complain thus: You heard I was planning a coup and
couldn't even ask me. What kind of friend are you? To this, Babangida
said he replied: I didn't believe it, or are you planning a coup? He said
Vatsa replied in the negative and the matter was forgotten until there
was evidence of the plot. Babangida said he instructed that Vatsa be
arrested and detained to prevent him from impeding investigation into
the matter.

Babangida argued: "However, Vatsa tried to escape through the air
conditioner hole. I couldn't understand why he was trying to escape if
he was not involved in a coup plot. But while watching the video of his
execution, I turned my eyes away when I saw him remove his watch and
ask a soldier to give his wife. I couldn't continue watching." Babangida
added that he couldn't retire or imprison Vatsa because he believed the
guy could still have planned a coup either in retirement or in prison.
"Rawlings did it in Ghana and you know Vatsa was very stubborn," IBB
said.

Omogui, however, lamented the tragedy that befell Vatsa: "Vatsa maintained
to the very end that the money was for farming. Others alleged, however,
that after being tortured for two days, Bitiyong implicated Vatsa by making
reference to certain private political conversations they had, which Vatsa
denied. But Vatsa was accused of harbouring "bad blood" against his
friend and classmate Babangida, dating back to the Buhari regime and
possibly earlier. He was also obliquely accused of reporting Babangida's
coup plot to Buhari before he left the country for pilgrimage along with
Major General Tunde Idiagbon in August, 1985.

Actions he later took as a Minister to accelerate many military
applications for certificates of occupancy for land in Abuja, came to
be viewed as efforts to buy the support of one or two of the plotters.
Rumours that a civilian had introduced him at a party as Nigeria's next
President were even aired. All of this was, of course, circumstantial. But
they took him to the stake, which was quite an anti-climax to the career
of a brilliant man who never took part in any coup in Nigeria. Indeed,

Mamman Vatsa was the first to go on air in Calabar to denounce the Dimka coup, and was later the Secretary of the Obada panel that tried Dimka and others in 1976. This little detail may have earned him some latent enmity in certain circles of the Army which later contributed to his death."

There is also a very strong belief that Vatsa may have been a victim of political intrigues because of his intellectual sagacity, being a writer and soldier-poet, and his significant indifference to the military politics at that time. In fact, his ordeal had attracted three leading Nigerian literary icons, Chinua Achebe, Wole Soyinka and John Pepper Clark Bekederemo, who had gone to plead with Babangida for clemency, only to be shocked by news of his execution few minutes after departing Dodan Barracks, venue of the meeting.

But in a swift reaction tainted with arrogance and insensitivity, Alhaji Shuibu Badeggi, Special Assistant on Public Communication to Governor Abdulkhadir Kure of Niger State and an aide of Babangida, stoutly defended the execution, claiming that a process found Vatsa and nine others culpable in the coup saga. According to him, Mrs. Vatsa's petition is baseless. "She should shut up. Shut up! If you commit a coup and you know the punishment is death, then you should face it. That's all. Those who plot a coup, when the coup fails, they die, simple. Talking about those saying all sorts of negative things about IBB, they are only out to score cheap political goals. Envy, grudge, that's all. It's envy and madness. Otherwise, if you thought 20 years ago that your husband had been wrongly accused of a coup plot and executed, why wait till now to demand that Babangida be punished? If anybody or group is using her to smear Babangida's image, then they have a problem because it is not Babangida who desperately wants to be president of Nigeria. It's we his supporters. There is nothing anyone of them can do in this and any other case."

This may be Badeggi's simple response to a complex issue which is already generating interest across the country. The day Badeggi's outburst came out, TheNEWS gathered; Mrs. Vatsa did not hold back her own ballistic missile. She reportedly said: "Anybody who says I am being used is a big fool. In the first place, my husband made Kure. As a Minister, my husband brought Nupe people to government. That was when Kure came to Abuja to work with my husband. If Kure was not made by my husband, would he be in a position to have an aide like the one talking rubbish? That aide should shut up 100 times. Nobody is sponsoring me. All I want is the matter to be opened up so that the whole world will witness the case.

Will justice be done in the Vatsa case?

CHAPTER SEVEN
IBB and Human Rights

The Babangida era did not only witness an unprecedented flourishing of pro-democracy and human rights groups; several civic organizations stepped up opposition to the regime when it mattered most. The SAP and transition programme provoked this healthy development.

Throughout its six-year tenure, the military government of General Ibrahim Babangida has relied on force to ensure its stay in power. In the process, the Babangida government has been responsible for the deaths of hundreds of students and others who demonstrated against its policies, the detention without trial of thousands of government critics, the silencing of opposition organizations and the erosion of the rule of law. In 1991, the continuation of those practices furthered the deterioration of an already crumbling civil society.

Babangida's tightly controlled program of transition to civilian rule, due to be completed by October 1, 1992, purports to be building a democracy. But the program has included a prohibition on all independent political parties and the denial of the right to vote to many other Nigerians. The government claimed that such controls were necessary to eliminate the ethnic, religious and regional violence that has plagued the country in the past. During 1991, however, escalating political violence and several outbreaks of religious riots in the north indicated that the old problems remain unsolved.

In December, thirteen former governors, senators and ministers were arrested for violating the ban on participation in politics by former politicians. They were accused of sponsoring candidates for state governorship elections and were ordered by the Transition to Civilian Rule Tribunal to remain in police custody until they reappear before the tribunal on January 16, 1992. However, the ban was lifted on December 18 with a government announcement that "the time has come when the old and new should mix, cooperate or compete."

Although President Babangida repeatedly declared his intention to complete the transition program on schedule, the growing violence has provoked official warnings that the transition is in danger of being derailed, and has encouraged speculation that the government might use the instability as an excuse to remain in power. Even if the military leaves office as planned, its success in manipulating the political system, weakening the courts and destroying such civilian institutions as the labor movement and student unions has ensured that the fragile new government will be vulnerable to future military influence. With less than a year to go, the government continues to rely on strong-arm tactics, and has refused to loosen its grip on civilian institutions.

Elections in 1990 had been conducted using an experimental method known as the "open ballot," in which voters line up behind photographs of their chosen candidates, rather than the secret ballot, as provided by Nigerian law. The possibilities for voter intimidation inherent in the open ballot system were obvious. In March 1991, the government announced that it would conduct an extensive nationwide opinion poll to canvas the views of Nigerians on the new voting system. Shortly thereafter, the government declared that, based on what was said to be the results of the poll, the open ballot would be used in all future elections.

The government continued its practice of ruling by military decrees, which are prohibited from being questioned by the courts. State Security (Detention of Persons) Decree 2 of 1984, the most widely abused and feared decree, provides for virtually unlimited detention without trial. In 1991, the government used Decree 2 to continue to hold relatives and acquaintances of suspected participants in the April 1990 coup attempt who are still at large. Those who remain in detention include Gloria Mowarin, the girlfriend of a suspected coup financier, whose release was ordered by the court on February 19. Pregnant at the time of her detention, she miscarried in her seventh month. Others include Gloria Awhirin and Rhoda Ackah, two sisters of Great Ogboru, the alleged coup leader. In June 1991, a High Court judge appealed to the federal government to order their immediate release on humanitarian grounds. One is nursing a baby. Dorah Mukoro, wife of Major Saliba Mukoro, an alleged coup participant, reportedly escaped from detention in September, along with her children. She gave birth in detention less than two months after her arrest.

As in past years, the government in 1991 was extremely sensitive to allegations of official corruption, which is widely recognized as one of Nigeria's most intractable problems. In the most talked-about case of the year, Jennifer Madike was arrested on January 10 for allegedly collecting a bribe from three men on the pretext that she was to deliver it to Fidelis Oyakhilome, then chair of the Nigerian Drug Law Enforcement Agency, to secure the release of two detained suspected drug dealers. She was later detained under Decree 2, amid rumors of the involvement of First Lady Maryam Babangida in the scandal. She was not produced in court until March 22, after numerous complaints filed by her lawyer, human rights activist Femi Falana, who is also president of the National Association of Democratic Lawyers and vice president of the Committee for the Defense of Human Rights. Madike was later charged with stealing and official corruption. Her cousin was arrested on April 17, and both women were subsequently charged with forgery in connection with a letter that the two claims were written to Madike by Mrs. Babangida. Madike became seriously ill in custody and is still denied access to her lawyer, despite several court orders.

One of the most damaging effects of military rule on the justice system has been the use of special tribunals. Lacking internationally recognized judicial safeguards, they hear a variety of cases considered by the government to be particularly sensitive, including cases of armed robbery, treason, corruption, drug trafficking and subverting the transition to civilian rule. Those convicted in some cases have no right of appeal. Others may be appealed to a Special Appeal Tribunal, but the appellate decisions must then be confirmed by the government. Until 1991, military officers sat on tribunals along with judges, but according to Decree 9 of 1991, tribunals now consist of one civilian judge. While a small improvement, this change does not address many of the fundamental problems of the tribunals, including a presumption of guilt, inadequate legal representation, disproportionately stiff sentences and strictly circumscribed provisions for appeal. In addition, the continued existence of a parallel court system weakens the authority of the regular courts.

Despite the removal of members of the military from the special tribunals, military tribunals are still used to try certain cases. Nine soldiers and two civilians, accused of involvement in the April 1990 coup attempt, were tried in secret before a military tribunal in September and October. According to the Civil Liberties Organization (CLO), a Nigerian human rights group, the suspects had been acquitted on similar charges in two previous trials before military tribunals and had been in detention for at least one year. They were denied counsel during their detention and were represented at the trial by army lawyers. The CLO filed a suit to restrain the trial and later learned that it had been concluded and that eight suspects had been sentenced to death and three to life imprisonment. Two weeks later, the government announced that, pursuant to its human rights policy, the death sentences were commuted to life imprisonment and the life sentences to ten years' imprisonment.

Corruption in the judiciary has worsened under the Babangida government which, at the highest levels, has shown a lack of respect for the courts. A government-sponsored candidate who headed the Nigerian Bar Association (NBA) from 1989 to 1991 assured a policy of nonconfrontation with the government. In March 1991, at the opening ceremony of the African Bar Association meeting in Abuja, the government announced a one million dollar "gift" to the NBA, much to the embarrassment of many Nigerian lawyers. On August 7, Attorney General and Minister of Justice Prince Bola Ajibola announced a plan to require licenses for all lawyers; many feared the plan would be used to exert greater control over the bar.

The last two military governments' hostility to academic pursuits has crippled universities throughout the country. In 1991, students were the targets of a renewed siege. The crackdown began in late May in response to an ultimatum issued by the banned student organization, the National Association of Nigerian Students. The ultimatum included demands for the reinstatement of suspended students, the unbanning of student unions on several campuses, and the undertaking of reforms in university administration. A number of students were arrested in the days before the ultimatum deadline, and protests occurred on campuses throughout the country on the day of the deadline. Two students in Lagos were killed during a campus clash between armed security agents and unarmed students. A government panel that was appointed to probe the riot headed by the chair of the college's governing council, echoed police claims that the use of lethal force had been justified.

In June, the police admitted holding two hundred students. Many have since been released, but others have been arrested. Seven student leaders who were arrested in late May and early June were detained under Decree 2; they were held in harsh conditions in two Lagos prisons until their release on August 21. Several of them were tortured. The students went on hunger strike and were not given medical attention despite serious medical complications. Upon their release, the students were forced to sign an "Undertaking to be of Good Conduct," which forbids them from commenting on their detention, suing the government for the detention, and participating in student protests.

The government has filed trumped-up criminal charges against a number of student activists for their role in demonstrations, including four at Obafemi Awolowo University (OAU) who appear to have been falsely accused of a murder. Students who were present when the murder at OAU occurred reported that the victim was killed by a mob and that the arrested students were not in the area at the time. Many others have been expelled from university. In response to the unrest, the Education Minister has threatened to require every student-union leader to undergo special training. He stated that the "leadership" program would "promote development-oriented student unionism as against the preaching and practicing of non-conformism."

Police brutality, a major issue in the country, has not been seriously addressed by the government, although it was an important focus of domestic human rights groups in 1991 and was a major point of criticism of the government's response to religious riots that broke out in the north on several occasions throughout the year. Security agents were widely accused of not acting quickly enough to contain the violence and of using excessive force once violence erupted. The inspector general of police warned that the police would "deal with" anyone who spread rumors about persistent unrest in Bauchi. In mid-October, General Babangida cut short his visit to the Commonwealth Heads of Government Conference in Zimbabwe when violence broke out in Kano. Hundreds were killed in several days of violence following the announcement of an open-air Christian revival. According to Christian refugees, security forces did not act decisively at the outset because of fears of provoking the Islamic leadership in the area. When violence escalated, the police fired indiscriminately at crowds, using live ammunition.

Femi Falana was harassed on numerous occasions, apparently because of his role as defense counsel for Jennifer Madike, whose case is described above. He was arrested on May 12, when security agents asked to see documents used in the defense of his client, and again on May 31, when he was accused of assisting student leaders in Nigeria at a time when he had been in the United States. In July, security officials threatened him with further action if he persisted with the Madike case. His passport was seized in October, when he was at the airport trying to leave the country to attend a meeting of nongovernmental human rights organizations from the Commonwealth countries. The meeting had been called to lobby the 1991 Commonwealth Heads of Government Conference, which was being held in Zimbabwe. He was questioned over the next two days about the Madike case and accused of being insufficiently patriotic because of his opposition to the government-sponsored candidacies of Nigerians to fill prestigious positions in the international arena.

The executive director of the Committee for the Defense of Human Rights, Clement Nwankwo, and the chairman of the CRPs's Lawyers Committee, Tayo Oyetibo, were questioned over a period of two days by officers of the Directorate of Military Intelligence about their defense of Dorah Mukoro, whose case is mentioned above, and the CRP's criticism of such government practices as rule by decree and the use of special tribunals. The CRP reported that the officers became angry when they refused to answer most of the questions. At a weekly press briefing in early October, Nigerian Vice President Aikhomu spoke out against human rights groups and the rights they seek to uphold.

It is easy for them to point accusing fingers on people, but have we ever asked in this country how these so called self-styled humanist organizations are funded? Who are their backers; their particular interest in our society? Today, we are fighting people responsible for illicit dealing in drugs, rapists, people who want to turn the society into a jungle, but the so-called human rights organizations in this country have interest to defend the rights of these enemies of society more than anything else. A few weeks later, after the CLO publicized the secret trial of coup suspects, the government made a public statement to the effect that something must be done to stop the CLO.

In November, the passport of human rights attorney Gani Fawehinmi was seized when he was on his way to London for medical treatment. No official reason was given for the action. Human rights attorney Alao Aka-Bashorun's passport, which was seized in 1990
has not yet been returned.

In 1991, students were the targets of a renewed siege. The crackdown began in late May in response to an ultimatum issued by the banned student organization, the National Association of Nigerian Students. The ultimatum included demands for the reinstatement of suspended students, the unbanning of student unions on several campuses, and the undertaking of reforms in university administration. A number of students were arrested in the days before the ultimatum deadline, and protests occurred on campuses throughout the country on the day of the deadline. Two students in Lagos were killed during a campus clash between armed security agents and unarmed students. A government panel that was appointed to probe the riot headed by the chair of the college's governing council, echoed police claims that the use of lethal force had been justified.

Seven student leaders who were arrested in late May and early June were detained under Decree 2; they were held in harsh conditions in two Lagos prisons until their release on August 21. Several of them were tortured. The students went on hunger strike and were not given medical attention despite serious medical complications. Upon their release, the students were forced to sign an "Undertaking to be of Good Conduct," which forbids them from commenting on their detention, suing the government for the detention, and participating in student protests. The government has filed trumped-up criminal charges against a number of student activists for their role in demonstrations, including four at Obafemi Awolowo University (OAU) who appear to have been falsely accused of a murder. Students who were present when the murder at OAU occurred reported that the victim was killed by a mob and that the arrested students were not in the area at the time. Many others have been expelled from university. In response to the unrest, the Education Minister has threatened to require every student-union leader to undergo special training. He stated that the "leadership" program would "promote development-oriented student unionism as against the preaching and practicing of non-conformism."

Labour: a radical wing of the Nigerian Labour Congress, led by Mallam Ciroma, was in control of labour affairs when Babangida came to power. Well-informed about the role of Labour in pre and post- independent Nigeria, his overall strategy was to replace the radical wing with a moderate, if not conservative, faction. The killing of four students of the Ahmadu Bello University (ABU) Zaria in May 1986 and the subsequent solidarity march against the genocide - as a section of the Press called it - provided an alibi for the first attack. NLC headquarters in Lagos was sealed up; it was there accused of provocation and insensitivity to the national economic emergency; the executive of the Congress was dissolved and a sole administrator appointed to run its affairs.

By 1988, there was a massive infiltration of the Union. At its national convention in Jos, government sponsored a group led by Shamang which, in one fell swoop, paid by cash, union dues it could not pay in two years. Having.13 been used to cause schism within the NLC, Shamang withdrew from public consciousness. Comrade Pascal Bafyau, leader of the Railways Union whose members' economic woes were well-known under Babangida, became the president of the Congress. He was very close to the General; indeed several of the Congress' policy somersaults both on trade union and political matters, before and after June 12 annulment, could be traced to Bafyau's extensive informal networks with the military regime.

Some of the Union's political options were bizarre: establishment of a political association that sought licence from the regime to participate in Third Republic politics; decision to support Bafyau's bid for Vice-president under Abiola with the attendant massive use of the ethnic and religious cards (Christian Northern minority from Adamawa state); indecisions whether or not to support calls by Campaign for Democracy for public disobedience immediately after the annulment (12) as well as vacillations in joining the oil unions - National Union of Petroleum and Natural Gas Senior Staff Association of Nigeria (PENGASSAN) - which fought for the recovery of Abiola's presidential mandate between July and September 1994.

The NLC's largely inclusive politics could not save it when the new military dictator, General Abacha, clamped down on NUPENG and PENGASSAN. Their executives, including that of NLC, were dissolved through that night broadcast on August 18, 1994.

The Bar Association: like in much of Africa, the Nigerian Bar Association was, for long, an extremely conservative union. Activist and radical lawyers were, unlike in the colonial period, few and far between. Highly hierarchical and unitary in outlook, NBA was run like a commandist movement until Alao Aka-Bashorun became its president. Well-known for his distaste for military rule, he rapidly closed the ranks of activist lawyers; and energized the association to begin to take a keener interest in judicial activism as against puerile legalism. He passed this new lease of life to Priscilla Kuye who did not disappoint.

The regime became alarmed. The government moved in at the Port Harcourt Convention (early 1993), which was attended for the first time in ten years by Gani Fawehinmi, the *opposant de toujours* of all Nigerian military regimes to date. It sponsored Bashir Dalhatu, until then relatively unknown, to contest the Association's presidency. The radical wing of the lawyers succeeded in stalemating the Convention when it appeared the government's protegé was on a victory course.

A measure of government's frustration with the outcome of the Convention was the setting up of a Body of Benchers - made up of the oldbreed, the Senior Advocates of Nigeria (SANs), now highly politicized and denied to activist lawyers - to resolve the internal crisis of the association. This did not help the regime, nor did a decree promulgated on the same matter permit it to find a solution acceptable to it before Babangida ouster. By August 1995, Kuye was still the *de facto* president of NBA, multiple court cases notwithstanding.

Women in Nigeria (WIN): It is interesting to note that this small group of Women activists in Nigeria has, despite its limited financial resources, persistently refused incorporation into the state-backed National Council of Women Societies (NCWS). Nor was it involved in the seeming large-scale inclusionary politics of the Better Life Programme (BLP) - more commonly called 'Better Life for Rural Women or rural dwellers' - initiated by Mrs Maryam Babangida. WIN, very serious with its gender project and emancipatory political engineering in respect of Nigerian women, apparently wishes to preserve its autonomy vis-a-vis the excesses and flamboyance of the programme, whatever its success in other areas .

In a fundamental sense, the continued occupation of the public space by the civic associations did not occur because of the Babangida regime, but in spite of it. Their tenacity of purpose - in large measure, their refusal not to succumb either to the politics of settlement or to cheap blackmail - and internal cohesion and solidarity in the face of a regime that was, at the count down to presidential elections in June 1993, highly intolerant of opposition and seemingly paranoid about clinging to power, was their greatest asset. As opposition mounted, Babangida sought to accommodate non-state actors in the last phase of the transition. This was sheer tokenism, however.

When, in his November 17, 1992 broadcast, Babangida announced the shift of handover date from January 2, 1993 to August 27, 1993, he also asked the Centre for Democratic Studies (CDS) - training school for future civilian leaders - to "put together, train and coordinate a group" made up of "representatives of professional organisations, labour unions, business organisations and human rights organisations" to monitor the presidential election. Bratton and de Walle (1994: 462) may therefore be right in arguing that because a military oligarchy is often shielded from reality, civic organisations have a lot to do: "... to make themselves heard - to penetrate the conspiracy of silence surrounding the supremo - ordinary citizens... [and] have little choice but to persist with protest and raise the volume of their demands".

IBB AND GANI FAWEHINMI

"If there is one man I respect, it is Gani, it sounds strange. I appreciate you that you have a strong conviction and fight for it consistently. This is the context in which I see Gani. I was a consistent evil and he was … a dogged fighter and I respect him for this. In fact there are three of them I respect like that. They are Gani, late (Professor) Awojobi and Dr. Yusuf Bala Usman. None of them says anything without doing his homework first." Ibrahim Babangida

The death of Gani was a great loss to Nigeria and the world. He was one of the few respected legal icons in Nigeria and the world, he stood up for what was right, even when standing alone. He was never afraid of detention, repression and harassment in the hands of Babangida and other successive rulers and dictators in Nigeria. He was detained more than any other Nigerian without usurping government like most of the khaki boys who overthrown democratically elected leaders and saw nothing good in democracy; but wish to become the country's president now after Gani and other patriotic few paid with their lives. Gani never looted the treasury of the country, he was rather a philanthropist whose love for the less privileged is worthy of emulation, yet, he was incarcerated rather than celebrated.

Gen Ibrahim Babangida never denied the patriotism of the fearless Gani but he couldn't help live with such an upright man with his (Babangida) stained garment. IBB recalled during his crocodile's tear; "I attended one meeting in 1984 when I was chief of staff, and we invited Gani. He said it the way it was. We were all in army uniform, but Gani blasted us, and we ended up clapping for him. Because he was quite fearless. He said it the way it is.
When we want to take decisions while I was head of state, we always took cognisance of what Gani might do. Because he would tear it to pieces and charge up the people against us".

It is on record that Babangida did not only detained Fawehinmi during his reign, he also instructed the elimination of the man systematically as confirmed by Gani, "I passed through dangerous regimes in Nigeria; especially the regime of Ibrahim Babangida".

71

Gain was never a smoker unlike some drug barons, pathetic hard drug smokers, we had as leaders; yet he die of lung cancer occasioned by regular incarceration and injection by the later.

Detained 17 times during Babangida's tenure

But by far, the Babangida administration had the singular honour of being the one that detained Gani the most – a record 17 times of the total 32 he was detained. Gani enjoyed relative "peace" after the detentions of 1978; a transition to civil rule programme instituted by the Obasanjo administration ushered in the civilian administration headed by Alhaji Shehu Shagari as President in October 1979.

It was short-lived however, by December 31, 1983, a military putsch which sent Shagari packing saw Geneal Muhammadu Buhari emerging Head of State. Buhari ruled only 20 months; in August 1985 General Ibrahim Babangida succeeded him, and a little over a year after, in 1987, Gani was back on familiar turf – in detention. His first detention under the IBB administration was at the dreaded Panti Police Station in 1987.

After his release, the following year, in 1988, Gani was to be detained at the same station three times. By the time Babangida left office in 1993, Gani had been in and out of detention seventeen times, and was detained in various locations from Lagos to Abuja and Maiduguri.

In his last interview before his death Gani narrated a discussion with one of the experts about his lung cancer: "I narrated everything to him, telling him my detention experiences.
"I asked whether that could have caused the lung cancer, through my experiences   which had accumulated over the years as a result of the detention or any poisons. One of them said it was possible. I am telling you I passed through dangerous regimes in Nigeria; especially the regime of Ibrahim Babangida.
"I also passed through dreaded Abacha regime. Those two regimes detained me horribly. The type of treatments meted to my body in those detentions could probably have contributed to this. They could not detect what caused this in England; they only know it is cancer. They also only know it was not caused by smoking. I couldn't give answer to what could

have caused this. This could be accumulation of the various evil misdeeds of the various governments.

"If the evil misdeeds of these military governments have caused it, well leave everything to God to judge".

The wife of the late luminary, Ganiyat also berated Ibrahim Babangida's crocodile tears over the passing of human rights lawyer. She revealed that her husband contracted cancer during one of his many incarcerations in the hands of the military dictator. "He knew he was going to die of the disease because it all started when he was locked up in prison during the Babangida military era till he eventually died."

Going further, Mrs. Fawehinmi said her late husband told her Babangida's agents kept injecting him with dangerous substances in detention with the aim of silencing him.

As far back as 1996, Gani had alleged that attempts were made on his life through the pumping of substances into his blood whenever he was detained by Babangida. He had revealed to Tell Magazine that such attempts on his life were affecting his eyes.

President of Campaign for Democracy, Dr. Joe Okei-Odumakin, believed such a step was not beyond the realm of what the former military dictator might have done. She said it is hard to exonerate Babangida from any medical problem Gani may have had because of the activist's record of fighting one of the most-wicked dictators in Nigeria's history.

Though Babangida had always won with the judiciary he helped to corrupt, Gani was always the champion at the peoples' parliament. Many believed that he had good cases against the former dictator but the dependent and partial Judiciary of Nigeria made it almost impossible to win Babangida, who most often fails to appear in court.

It must, indeed, be a relief to Babangida that the lawyer who he feared the most and who never gave up on tying the dicator to Dele Giwa's murder is gone.

Gani vs. Babangida

Apart from organizing peaceful rallies, street demonstrations against military dictatorship using his own personal resources, he utilizes the due process of the law and the machinery of justice to challenge what he perceives as illegal and unconstitutional policies, activities, and self-serving programmes of several governments which he considers inimical to the interest of the nation and the people of the country. He has filed more than three hundred of such cases in court. Some against Babangida and cohorts are as follows:

 # Suit No. M/87/88
Chief Gani Fawehinmi v. Akilu & Anor
An action to compel the Director of Public Prosecution of Lagos State to charge to Court Col. Halilu Akilu and Lt. Col. A.K. Togun (both top security officers in the government of General Babangida) for conspiracy to murder and the murder of Dele Giwa, the Editor-in-Chief of New swatch Magazine.

 # Suit No. FHC/L/CS/54/92
Chief Gani Fawehinmi & Anor. v. N.N.P.C & 4 Ors.
An action to force General Babangida's Military Government to render an account of all export earnings realized by Nigeria from the sale of Crude Oil during the Gulf War in 1991.

 # Suit No. LD/1092/92
Chief Gani Fawehinmi v. Babangida & Ors
An action to challenge the use of public funds by the wife of the Head of State for activities not recognized by law.

 # Suit No. CS/53/92
Chief Gani Fawehinmi vs. Central Bank of Nigeria & 4 Ors
An action challenging the illegal 100% devaluation of Nigerian currency on March 5, 1992.

 # Suit No. FHC/L/CS/67/92
Chief Gani Fawehinmi vs. Gado Nasko & Anor
An action to compel the Minister of the Federal Capital Territory and the Federal Capital Territory Authority to render account of all public funds received and expended by them between 1975 and 1992 which hitherto they had not rendered.

 # Suit No. M/132/93
Chief Gani Fawehinmi v. Ibrahim Badamasi Babangida

An action to challenge the illegality, illogicality, uncertainty, absurdity and incongruity contained in a number of decrees made by General Babangida which showed that some decrees had the same number with different dates and different titles.

 # Suit No. ID/2619/93
Chief Gani Fawehinmi vs. Shonekan
An action challenging the Interim National Government of Shonekan and exposing the unconstitutionality of his illegal regime.

 # Suit No. M/551/93
Chief Gani Fawehinmi vs. Attorney General of the Federation.
An action calling the court's attention to the illegality of General Babangida's signing a decree into law after he had ceased to be a Head of State and Commander-in-Chief of the Armed Forces.

PRISON LIFE
Gani spent a large part of his life in detention for challenging the tyrants like Babangida and cohorts; such experiences include:

DETENTIONS:

Police Headquarters, Kaduna, 1969

Jos Police Station, 1969

Ilorin Police Station, 1969

Police Headquarters, Lagos, 1969

Police Headquarters, Lagos 1972 (twice)

C. I. D. Alagbon, Lagos, 1978

Inter-Centre Detention Outpost, Lagos, 1978

Ikoyi Police Station, 1978

Panti Police Station, Lagos, 1987

Panti Police Station, Lagos, 1988 (three times)

Police Station Ikeja, 1988

Panti Police Station, Lagos, 1989 (twice)

Ikoyi Police Station, 1989

SSS Cell Maiduguri, 1989

SSS Cell Awolowo Road, Ikoyi 1991

C. I. D. Police Station Ikoyi, 1992

Police Station Wuse Abuja, 1992

Inter-Centre Cell, Lagos 1993

SSS Awolowo Road, Ikoyi, 1993

C. I. D. Police Station Ikoyi, 1993

Police Station Wuse Abuja, 1993

Police Headquarters, Abuja, 1993

Panti Police Station, Lagos, 1994

F. I. I. B. Alagbon, Ikoyi, Lagos 1994 (Once)

Panti Police Station, Lagos, 1995 (Twice)

SSS Shangisha Cell Lagos, 1995 (Once)

SSS Shangisha Cell Lagos, 1996 (Once)

PRISON EXPERIENCE

Kaduna Prison, 1969

Gombe Prison, 1969 – 1970

Ikoyi Prison, 1978

Gashua Prison, 1989

Nigerian Prison Ikoyi, 1990

Nigerian Prison Kuje, 1992

Nigerian Prison Kuje, 1993 and Nigerian

CHAPTER EIGHT
IBB and drug

Nobody knows more about the international drug trade better than Alain Labrousse. The author of the best selling book 'Geopolitics of Drugs' and former Director of the Geopolitical Watchdog on Drugs (OGD), clearly identified Nigeria's former military rulers and diplomats as drug barons. In an authoritative report still posted on the web site of the Canadian Parliament on the drug trade in Africa, Labrouse marks out Ibrahim Babangida, Nigeria's former self-appointed president, as one of the drug-dealing dictators in Africa.

The report says: "The international community has long considered Nigeria a narco-state: the United States put it on the list of 'decertified' countries between 1994 and 1999, and the Dublin Group, consisting mainly of the European countries, unfearingly called it a 'narco-regime'. Its President, General Babangida, and his wife have been suspected of engaging in cocaine trafficking, along with numerous other military officers." Apart from Babangida and his wife, Maryam, top military brass and members of the diplomatic corps are some others identified in the international investigation of the drug ring that prospered from the early 1980s through the mid-1990s.

Major Orkar, whose unsuccessful coup plot was the most successful attempt to dispose Babangida of power, also alleged that there was drug dealing going on during the regime of the dictator. Said Orkar: "I, Major Gideon Orkar, wish to happily inform you of the successful ousting of the dictatorial, corrupt, drug baronish, evil man, deceitful, homo-sexually-centered, prodigalistic, un-patriotic administration of General Ibrahim Badamasi Babangida." Since Orkar called IBB a drug baron, many Nigerians have quietly accepted it as a fact.

In Labrousse's report, he claimed: "The United States in particular raised questions about the former Minister of Foreign Affairs, Tom Ikimi, who made use of the services of the director of a Lagos newspaper who frequently traveled abroad to distribute cocaine and heroin imported from Latin America and Asia among the members of his network of resellers around the world.

"Another soldier long involved in drug trafficking was Major Hamza Al-Mustapha, head of the feared Abacha Security Service (SSS), who carried on his dealings by diplomatic pouch. His wife, of Arab origin, coordinated a ring in the Gulf countries. "A former head of Nigeria's permanent delegation to the United Nations was also apparently involved. Nigerian top officials' dealing in drugs under the cover of diplomacy is characteristic of dictatorships around the world, especially in Africa, where Mobutu Sese Seko of Zaire and Charles Taylor of Liberia are known to have treaded the same path.

In the case of Equatorial Guinea, diplomats belonging to the president's family or clan used the diplomatic pouch and their immunity to engage in cocaine and heroin traffic around the world. Tens of them have been arrested over the past two decades, particularly in Spain. The family of Mozambican President Chissano has also been involved a number of times in cocaine cases. But in the case of Babangida, he has been lucky never to have been caught.

The military connection in the drug trafficking business is particularly noteworthy. Military officers have for long been suspected of coordinating the drug trade. The burning of the Ministry of Defence Building in Lagos during Babangida's regime, during which The Sunday Guardian showed IBB smiling right in front of the burning edifice, was believed to have been official arson executed to hide some sensitive information about the trade.

The only case that has been widely linked to Babangida, which many thought could have exposed him is that of Gloria Okon, a Nigerian lady alleged to have been his courier and said to have died in detention but believed to have been resettled in anonymity. It is widely accepted that the murdered journalist, Dele Giwa, was about to unravel the mysterious disappearance of Gloria Okon when he was killed in circumstances tied around Babangida's neck. Babangida has refused to answer charges of his involvement in the bombing of Dele Giwa, and has used every available legal means to refuse to testify. The Oputa panel set up by the Obasanjo administration to uncover the misdeeds of the past regimes submitted that Babangida has a case to answer regarding Dele Giwa's death.

Starting in the early 1980s, Nigerian traffickers began to gain prominence as they swallowed condoms full of heroin and transported them to European countries and the United States. They sourced the drug from Thailand, Pakistan and India, transited through Ethiopia and Kenya and Central Africa and headed for the Western countries. . At the same time, Nigerians traveled to South America to pick up cocaine destined for European markets and, starting in 1994, for South African markets. According to the World Customs Organization (WCO), Nigerian drug traffickers were involved in 1,200 cases in the world between 1991 and 1995.

According to Alain Labrousse, "It was first thought that the Nigerian organizations were mainly family or clan-based. According to various sources, however, particularly American, there is what could be called a genuine Mafia in Nigeria: "drug barons", supported by "under-barons", who in turn have their own groups of couriers. In this organization, three leaders head up 85 cells of approximately 40 members. In those cells, a "lieutenant" apparently commands six to 20 "soldiers". The structure is found in the organization of the Nigerian rings in the United States. Operation Tonga, carried out by European police in 1995 and 1996, also showed that there were links between the Colombian Mafia, the Neapolitan Camorra and the Nigerian rings.

Similarly, Nigerians are well established in most Eastern countries. Their "bridgeheads" are most often scholarship students from communist regimes who have remained penniless since the political upheavals resulting from the fall of the Berlin Wall. Nigerian traffickers are thus the only native African groups on the most wanted lists of the law enforcement agencies of the rich countries, together with international criminal organizations and the Colombian, Chinese, Turkish, Pakistani and, more recently, Kosovar drug rings.

An estimated 35-40% of the entire heroin coming into the United States is brought by Nigerian couriers. In 1989, the United States and Nigeria established a joint Counter-Narcotics Task Force. Lack of cooperation by Nigerian authorities in combating the drug trafficking problem led to a decision by the Clinton Administration in March 1998, as in 1994 and 1996, to put Nigeria on the State Department's list of non-cooperative drug trafficking nations.

The administration of Buhari and Idiagbon saw the grave danger posed by the drug trade, and it waged a very serious war against it. It killed by firing squad two Nigerians caught with drugs while attempting to take them overseas. It had been rumored that if Babangida had not staged his coup at the time he did, he was under the radar for his drug business and would have been arrested.

When IBB took power, Nigeria began to feign combating drug trading. While he put a stop to death sentence for drug trafficking, Babangida set up the National Drug Law Enforcement Agency, which recruited its first set of graduates in 1990. Since then, even the agency has been involved in the drug business. In 1992, drugs seized by the agency continued to disappear even under the oversight of the court in its own premises. The NDLEA ridiculed IBB's drug fight. And no arrested trafficker has given away the name of the boss so far. According to the U.S. Drug Enforcement Agency (DEA), Nigeria's anti narcotic efforts remain "unfocused and lacking in material support."

While it has never been officially confirmed, reports by some Nigerian newspapers in 1993, at the time when Babangida was disgraced out of power, claimed that the Evil Genius was wanted by the US government for drug trafficking. It was said that that was why Babangida has not stepped on American soil since he left power.

So, was Babangida a drug baron? There is sufficient suspicion and information, especially outside of the country to link him with drug trafficking in the 1980s and the early 1990s. However, because he has always avoided circumstances that could make him give answers to those allegations, he has never been pinned down. His failure to travel to a country like the United States, where he is believed to be wanted, adds fuel to speculations about his past. Perhaps, if he were to stop raising legal obstacles to the murder of Dele Giwa, a chance to question him about Gloria Okon may bring up the most closely guided open secret of his regime.

It was alleged that he sent letter bomb to Dele Giwa that snuffed the life of that great man out of this life. Dele was investigating the drug deal that involved Gloria Okon and Miriam Babangida and this man had to stop the investigative journalist through a letter bomb. All sorts of calamitous events kept rolling out at the time, including the arrest of one Ikuomola for trying to smuggle a large consignment of cocaine out of the country. He indicted a son of one of the Dantatas and they were both tried and sentenced to death. The Dantata family mounted pressure on the Supreme Military Council to commute the sentence to life. The issue heightened the division among the Supreme Military Council members, with the Gloria Okon's high ranking military benefactor, siding with the Dantatas naturally.

Idiagbon insisted that if poor people found with cocaine could be punished with death sentence, why should the rich and affluent be spared? Idiagbon also wanted the lawyer, (a Rivers state chap who had received some four million naira as legal fees on the case at the time), to be shot along with the drug barons for benefiting from the evil.

The schism between Idiagbon and Babangida totally paralyzed the Supreme Military Council and it could no longer function. Idiagbon forced compulsory leave on Babangida, under close surveillance with tapped telephone lines and all.

CHAPTER NINE
IBB and the press

With the Judiciary, the Press represents a very important pillar of democracy globally. Babangida knew this and sought to chain it - not quite successfully - as he did for the Judiciary. The travails of the Nigerian Press under Babangida came from two major sources, the one a direct consequence of journalists' naivety in rallying around Babangida in his euphoric early days in power, the other, derivative of the character of ownership.

Perhaps understandably, goodwill for Babangida after his coup de force came most from the Press – in particular its so-called Lagos- Ibadan axis. He had quickly annulled Decree 4 of 1984 by which two journalists of

The Guardian - arguably the country's most liberal newspaper, some of its workers were jailed by the Buhari regime. The decree made it an offence to publish any story embarrassing to government officials even if the story were true. The two journalists, Tunde Thompson and Nduka Irabor (who would later become the Chief Press Secretary of Aikhomu and linked with the announcement of the June 12 annulment), were not only given State pardon; their jail record was also officially nullified.

Few journalists countenanced the survival of another notorious decree - Number 2 of 1984 - by which the chief of General Staff could detain, without formal charges, anyone deemed to be a security risk. This instrument was invoked later to undertake large-scale search of media houses; to arrest and detain journalists and close down media.12 houses. Few of the latter, whose numbers kept on growing, were spared of the regime's aversion to criticisms of its policy programmes.

The killing by a parcel bomb (a dangerous and sophisticated innovation in Press-military relations) of Dele Giwa editor-in-chief of the country's first weekly magazine, Newswatch, in October 1986 marked a turning point for both ill and good. While several media house became muted in their critique, a few others, in particular Abiola's African Concord pursued their well-beaten opposition path. African Concord would later fall after a face-off with government led to its closure and its radical journalists left in droves, having refused to apologize to the General. A team of the break-aways, under the leadership of Bayo Onanuga, African Concord's former editor, subsequently founded The News and Tempo, two weeklies that rapidly became objects of severe repression by the regime. There was also Tell magazine, radical and punchy too. It was founded by a splinter group from Newswatch.

The character of private newspaper proprietorship in Nigeria has often assailed the radical credentials of most journalists. The point is this: the Nigerian reading public, more sophisticated as the year go by, prefer an anti-government Press; not necessarily because they await a violent change too suddenly, but because that is the only avenue to know the truth. Radio and television stations are, save for isolated pockets, government-owned. The reading public is sometimes disappointed because many newspaper owners are government contractors. Thus, while there is a formal autonomy from the State, there is an informal immersion - admittedly in different degrees and therefore with unequal repercussions - in the State's informal, patronage network. Under the Babangida regime, this phenomenon became highly developed and visible.

The Babangida regime promulgated Decree 43, which prescribed new registration guidelines for all newspapers and was designed to control the press and silence its criticism of the regime. The guidelines require the payment of registration fees of approximately $10,000 and approval of a registration application by a newspaper registration board whose members are appointed by the Secretary for Information and Culture. The Decree lays out tough penalties, including prison terms and fines, for the circulation of unregistered newspapers and publication of false statements. It requires also that every issue display the names and addresses of its owners, publishers, and printers. Registration must be renewed annually.

The Nigerian press, which for years was regarded as the most vibrant in Africa, was increasingly under attack during the administration. In 1991, the government continued its policy of closing down newspapers and arresting journalists who reported on such sensitive topics as corruption and student demonstrations. Government attacks on the press included:

•Three newspapers in Lagos owned by John West Publications were shut down in March for thirteen days for what was described as "embarrassing publications" against the president and his wife, relating to the Jennifer Madike case described above. Under the heading "IBB, Maryam [Babangida] named in Jennifer's deal," the offending story, which appeared in the Lagos Evening News, reported the contents of a letter purportedly written by the chair of the Drug Law Enforcement Agency in which he justified the need to detain Madike under Decree 2. The paper's editor and news editor were arrested and detained for a few days.

•On May 29, the Lagos State government temporarily closed down the Guardian, a daily, after its coverage of the student killings in Lagos described above. Four journalists and two office assistants were arrested. The paper reopened nearly two weeks later. The journalists and assistants were released the next day without charge.

•William Keeling, a correspondent for the British daily Financial Times, was expelled from Nigeria and declared persona non grata. The government accused him of writing inaccurate articles "ostensibly to cause mischief and disharmony among Nigerians and between Nigeria and the rest of the world." The government's statement cited an article in which Keeling had accused the government of not reporting about half of the extra five billion dollars that it was estimated to have earned from higher oil prices during the Gulf war.

CHAPTER TEN
IBB and education

On May 30 1989, Nigerian University students embarked on what was called SAP riot, but it was a peaceful demonstration to liberate ourselves from perpetual economic slavery of Babangida and his colonial masters. The then Gbenga Olawepo (NANS PRO) and a student of University of Lagos, was in South Korea to represent Nigerian Students at a world conference. Babangida had sent his SSS as Nigerian students, but the then Olawepo went and presented the true situation of Nigeria at the conference. This was embarrassing to Babangida, who declared Olawepo wanted, at that time Gbenga Komolafe, Student Union Speaker of University of Ibadan was also wanted. Olawepo was eventually arrested when he came back to the country; Komolafe too was arrested at Dugbe in Ibadan. Both were first detained at Shangisa, but got transferred to Kirikiri when they caught their middleman who went to deliver message to Mr. Femi Falana. These guys were in detention for 6 months or more than that. At this time, Babangida shut 6 Universities for their involvement in the Anti-SAP demonstration. The Universities were not opened until November 1989 from May 30. This actually marked the beginning of irregular academic calendar in our Universities, and it also greatly affected the exchange programme with foreign universities, many professors left our universities and things have not been the same since then.

The Nigeria library also suffered serious negative effect with the introduction of the Structural Adjustment Programme. According to J.C. Ogugua in his article titled, *The Effects of the Structural Adjustment Programme on Nigerian Public Libraries* include;

•Large price increases for essential services and for books and other materials (up to 400% between 1985 and 1987; a greater percentage of increase since 1987);
•Government appropriations for public libraries have risen very slightly, or actually fallen, since SAP began; for example the subvention to Imo State Library Board experienced a real–currency decline of about 70% in appropriations between 1984 and 1992;

•Building projects have been delayed or cancelled;
•Maintenance of facilities is minimal;
•Binding of newspapers and journals has been abandoned by most libraries;
•Theft and mutilation of materials have increased, as a result of costs too high for individual purchases; and,
•Vacant positions have been left unfilled.

To librarians — and, it appears, to the rest of the Nigerian people (except for the wealthy class) — SAP is proving to be a hardship. Inflation consumes the small salaries that most people earn. Crime, disease, strikes and lockouts and widespread hunger are the signs of failure in SAP. At the very least, the government ought to remove the import duties on books and other library requirements, so that some flow of materials can resume. It would not involve too great a cost to increase maintenance of library facilities. Key vacancies ought to be unfrozen. Library managers also have the responsibility of finding ways to save money, by seeking supplementary ways to acquire materials.

The major recurring theme in the ASUU-Babangida regime confrontation was the poor State of university education in the country. ASUU argued that this was due to the combination of three factors: inadequate funding; lack of internal autonomy and poor remuneration of Nigerian universitaires. The first major crisis that prompted government's proscription of the union in July 1988 (it would be recognised again in August, 1990 and reproscribed in August 1992) was ASUU's rejection of an apparent government decision to de-emphazise university education.

This was a position of the IMF as canvassed at the meeting of Vice-Chancellors of African Universities in Harare in 1986. The argument was that only pre-university and technical education was cost - effective in Africa. Continued struggle on the three dossiers mentioned above prompted the new proscription of ASUU but it then made little sense because the union had become better organized and more radicalized. An Association of University Teachers (AUT) rapidly replaced it nation-wide. Whilst still withholding recognition of ASUU, Babangida's regime was forced to sign a historic agreement with the union on the three dossiers on September 3, 1992. Eventually, an ASUU member could trace Babangida's precipitated departure from Aso Rock partly to ASUU's "role in destroying the regime's myth of invincibility and refusing to be bought" (O. Ibeanu, 1993: 8-9).

Under Babangida regime, NANS, like ASUU, was proscribed and deproscribed several times, but it continually defied the regime, meeting in Ibadan, its headquarters, and in other major cities of the country, often with the knowledge of either university authorities or state security services (SSS). It stage anti-SAP riots of 1988, 1989 and 1991 which drew support from a cross-section of other non-State associations nation-wide.

CHAPTER ELEVEN
IBB and Ken Saro Wiwa, JOS: the blood of the minority

The administration of Babangida never listened to the plight of minority; rather, he chose to oppress them. The administration created the present day Jos crisis. He allegedly favoured the Hausas, who are not the true descendent of Jos, using the instrument of violence to suppress the the land owners; today fight is just an escalation of what the evil genius created years back. Millions of lifes have been lost to this mindless thought of the 1990s.

In 1993, 300,000 Ogoni marched peacefully to demand a share in oil revenues and some form of political autonomy. They had formed an organization called MOSOP (Movement for the Survival of Ogoni People), and they also asked the oil companies to begin environmental remediation and pay compensation for past damage. They were a minority and felt that they were not being given their human rights, and they were being tortured just so the country could make money off the oil that was on their land.

This started a lot of opposition from the government, and the leader, Ken Saro-Wiwa was imprisoned on several occasions. In November of 1993, Abacha took over the government, and this is when the real trouble started for the Ogonis. The military started terrorizing Ogoniland with arrests, rapes, executions, burnings and lootings. It is believed that the Shell oil company was working with the government, and that is part of the reason there were many protests worldwide to boycott them. In May

1994 Saro-Wiwa was abducted from his home and jailed along with other MOSOP leaders and charged with the murder of four Ogoni leaders. By this time, the world was involved in the issue, and dismissed these charges as fraudulent. While Ken was in detention, he was denied legal or medical help (which if you do a lot of reading, is unfortunately common in Nigerian prisons), and he had 4 heart attacks while in jail.

On October 31, 1995, the military government tried him and the other 8 people, and found them guilty of the murder of the 4 Ogoni people. The sentence immediately drew an international outcry by concerned persons and organizations, including Earthlife Africa, Amnesty International, Friends of the Earth, Greenpeace, the United Nations, and others. They urged the government to spare the lives of the environmentalists, and they called on Shell to intervene, but on November 10, 1995, Saro-Wiwa and the others were executed anyway. Their execution resulted in more international outcry, and Nigeria was almost immediately suspended from the Commonwealth.

The names of those executed were
- Ken Saro-Wiwa
- Saturday Dobee
- Barinem Kiobel
- Paul Levura
- Nordu Eawo
- Felix Nuate
- Daniel Gbokoo
- John Kpuinen
- Baribor Bera

Nigeria was suspended from the Commonwealth almost immediately, and sanctions were placed against the country, including oil sanctions, which accounted for over 90% of the nation's exports. Also, Shell had to halt its operations in Ogoni territory.

CHAPTER TWELVE
IBB and his political value

To all appearances, the Babangida military regime in Nigeria (27 August 1985 to 26 August 1993) was a mere military oligarchy in the sense of the term as used by Michael Bratton and Van de Walle (1994: 479 ff). Elements of the oligarchy include lack of concentration of power exclusively in the hands of the personal leader; collective decision-making by soldier-rulers and civilian technocrats and advisers, and an initial openness that permits debates and the use of objective yardsticks in policy evaluation. Such an oligarchy was present in the military presidency of General Babangida during the euphoric early months of his regime. It soon began to metamorphose into strategic designs towards personal rulership. Its ultimate degeneration was an attempt which meets Bratton and de Walle's conclusions that "personal rulers are unlikely to initiate political liberalization from above or relinquish power without a struggle; they have to be forced out"

The major thesis is that the Babangida personal rulership project was designed to accumulate all powers and dispense all patronage for as long as possible. This was to develop later, as the Babangida regime became more repressive and muscular, both qualitatively and quantitatively. State repression did not deaden non-state actors and institutions in Nigeria, implying that the Nigerian State under General Babangida had less freedom from societal pressures. Thus, if Nigeria's first-ever military president did not eventually become a tin-pot, sit-tight dictator, it was not for want of attempt, but in view of superior non-military forces in the Civil Society and fissures within the military organization, between, principally, political soldiers and professional soldiers.

In the beginning: General Babangida's *Révolution de Palais*

When General Ibrahim Babangida seized the reins of power with a classical palace coup on August 27, 1985, there was a general relief amongst Nigerians. The 'celebration', as in the past, was not to welcome the arrival of a new military junta but to celebrate the demise of the ancient regime. This is a politico-psychological behaviour of the Nigerian political animal, often misunderstood by many an Africanist. The departure of a government is often seen, rightly or wrongly, as a decisive opportunity for a new beginning towards nation-building and development.

General Babangida's ascendancy to the *magistrature suprême* brought something additional in its trail, however. In contradiction to the grim-faced, unsmiling General Buhari and his deputy General Idiagbon, Babangida brought smiles as well as a personal aura and warmth to the Nigerian political landscape. There was something seemingly arresting about him which was transmitted to the nation and the people by the media, in particular the press, namely, no matter how bad the Nigerian economic crisis, people could still afford a smile whilst tackling it.

By throwing open the prison gates for many of the political detainees; unchaining the press through a repeal of Decree 4 of 1984 as well as promising respect of fundamental human rights, Babangida rapidly concluded his initial political rites of legitimacy and support building. Before the close of that year, virtually all non-State groups and interests had, either explicitly or implicitly, indicated their willingness to give the regime the benefit of the doubt; fence-sitters were few and far between. The alleged Vasta coup - even though apparently only at the intention stage - of December 1985 further knitted the people to 'their' General. The latter had everything going for him. By the end of 1986, the regime had a favourable end-of-the-year review from two American Africanists.

"Under Babangida", observed L. Diamond and D. Galvan (1987: 75), "Nigeria has permitted domestic human rights groups (such as the Human Rights Committee of the Nigerian Bar Association and international ones (such as Amnesty International) to operate freely". Even though at the next page, the authors averred that "...as Nigeria made democratic progress in 1986, it also showed signs of deepening authoritarianism", the warning could easily have been ignored.

Similarly, in the Politburo and general political orientation debate in the country in 1986, a sizeable pocket of informed Nigerians, in re-echoing Dr Azikiwe's dyarchy thesis, may have been persuaded that the Babangida junta had some inherent qualities that could facilitate a civil polity and an 'enduring democracy' - a term the regime would use very often later. This is an educated guess from a highly charismatic and euphoric early period of theregime.

Thus, when the political transition programme (PTP) commenced, Babangida could hold all the aces on account of the experience of the short - lived Second Republic. He could claim that his vision of transition through institutional development as against mere legal changes required more time than the first transition supervised by General Obasanjo. Peter Koehn (1989: 418) has argued that the latter dealt more with "formal structural rearrangements or re-alignments". In the process, it "avoided dealing with the difficult matter of political culture, political economy and mass mobilisation in official structures and electoral processes". Babangida could, and indeed did, plead for a prolonged transition on this basis.

On the economic Structural Adjustment Programme (SAP) introduced in June 1986, Oyovbaire argued that it would help the democratic agenda of the regime. While claiming an initial success, in terms of SAP trimming down to a "useable size the bloated aspirations, undue expectations and rootless values which the oil boom of the post-civil war era created for the giddy existence of democracy in Nigeria", he foresaw the regime's democratic experiment stabilizing, but only if the attempt "to keep to shape the Nigerian society, economy and polity" subsisted. Oyovbaire was rigorous enough, however, to emphasise that his conclusions were "not oblivious of the possibilities of disruptive forces". Only that, when they did come, they were not from the sources Oyovbaire thought.

It would seem, by advantage of hindsight, that Oyovbaire and his colleagues took Babangida too seriously, at any rate more seriously than he took himself. One could therefore pardon non-insiders when they accord much premium to the president's grand public rhetorics. For instance, Narasingha P. Sil (1993: 61) writing on the regime's privatization programme, claims that "the point that is often overlooked by the critics of privatisation is that the government - preferred purchasers are "groups and institutions like trade unions, universities, youth organisations, women societies, local governments and state investment companies" - a direct reference to a Babangida speech. He adds that "these do not constitute the traditional accumulating bourgeoisie - organisational or entrepreneurial - but represent "groups and individuals who could not otherwise afford to purchase these companies"". In the same vein, William Reno (1993: 67) believes that the primary goal of the regime's economic and political reforms was to "break the grips of former first... and Second Republic politicians on State institutions and resources". Furthermore, he seems to believe that the president's overall economic objective was to impose "a State-defined rationality of economic efficiency upon elites in order to promote economic development and service the country's external debt obligations". He claims that "such a task requires political discipline to constrain elites from unregulated access to inefficient rent-seeking activity" (p.69).

Personal Rulership or Recomposing and Shrinking the Political Market

The Babangida regime, perhaps also the man, was an enigma of sorts: while public rhetorics were an indefinite discourse of sorts on democracy, nationhood and stability, they also often were thinly veiled double-speak. As late as mid-May 1993, Babangida reiterated, for the umpteenth time, Military's imminent dis-engagement from formal politics. The occasion was a graduation ceremony of the elite War College in Lagos:

"The military's commitment to withdraw to the barracks is irrevocable. With the countdown to the elections in June, all seems set for the conclusion of the experimental political journey we commenced in 1986. By August, this administration would be ready to hand over the baton of leadership to an elected president".

He even warned the ranks-and-file of the military not to be found "on the other side of the democracy barricade"; rather they should get prepared for "a democratic civilian succession to which they must be subordinate". Yet, in the same speech, Babangida returned to his old "custodian theory' of the military by which the latter could intervene at any moment to rescue the nation's sovereignty, territorial integrity, security and stability from perceived external and internal threats. He even claimed that in the country's "peculiar situation" - another beloved term - "the boundary between civil and military society is not clear-cut".

Babangida's political practices were even more intriguing. The strategic design was an intricate balancing of inclusion-exclusion; competition-participation in order to better control human and material resources and entrench personal power.

The promised new socio-political and economic order was to emerge; we have alluded to this, through the tandem transition programme - SAP. Yet the first component and, logically, to a lesser extent, the second were largely dirigiste and commandist; stifling initiatives and innovations, muzzling opposition and eventually, shrinking the politico-democratic space. As the years dragged on, it became increasingly clear that a tightly controlled political programme is the inescapable hand maiden of a largely deregulated economy, under the close surveillance of the military president.

The close tackling debuted with the Politburo, constituted in January 1986 to organise nation-wide consultations with Nigerians on the way forward politically. This is a well-researched period of Nigerian political history and therefore details need not detain us (see, inter alia, Rotimi A.O. and J.O. Ihonvbere, 1994: 669-689; Ihonvbere, 1990: 601-626; Agbese P.O. and G.K. Kieh, 1992: 19-35; Agbese, 1991: 293-311; 1990: 23-44; W. Reno: 1993: 66-87; P.M. Lewis, 1994: 323-40; O. Oyediran and A. Agbaje, 1991; K. Amuwo, 1990, 1992, 1993). I only seek to underline a few issues.

Whilst the 17-man body was composed of men and women, qualified both in character and learning to do the job, the use to which the report was put was entirely beyond them. Yet, it was a great moral, professional and political risk for the members - in particular, the many political scientists and the only self-avowed communist on board, Dr Edwin Madunagu of the respected newsdaily, *The Guardian*. The latter was later dropped because of 'extremist' and 'uncooperative' views and attitudes. Two things are interesting here. One, the report of the bureau was almost ready while sessions were still on nation-wide. Two, all the members were promised involvement in the management of the ensuing transition politics. Only about three or four members did not benefit from the promise. The personal loyalty of some of the most visible future managers of the transition programme to Babangida was thereby guaranteed.

The two-party State - erroneously referred to as a two-party system - admittedly recommended by the Politburo but imposed in form and substance by the regime was a subtle beginning of personal rulership. Part of the rationalization for a two-party State was, in a fundamental sense, a throw-back to the pre 1979 recivilianization process, namely, multi-partism may revive old demons of ethnicity and regionalism. The 1979 constitution has settled this issue by prescribing, as Douglas Rimmer (1994: 99-100) recently reminds us, that "parties should not by their names or emblems be identified with any ethnicity, region or religion and that the governing body of each should contain members of the States of the federation". For a regime that elevated itself to high political theology so-called settled issues in the body politic (federalism, secularism etc), this was a curious decision. Henceforth, highly susceptible to easy infiltration and manipulation, both parties operated in practice "as might have been foreseen as coalitions of aspirants to political office innocent of any ideological convictions" (Rimmer, *ibid.*).

In order to facilitate understanding of the dialectical relations between the management of the transition program and the operation of the economy and how these shaped the personal political agenda of Babangida, I identified three levels of analysis. These are (a) The president's personal charm and warmth; (b) the Constitution of an extensive patronage system and (c) the Politics of repression. A binding thread is the overall political objective of the military president as he moved adroitly from one level of operation to the other; as he re-jigged and juggled his cabinet and the political landscape of States and local governments; as he controlled oil rents and used them to make and unmake strategic and tactical alliances and as he wielded carrot and stick before conscientious objectors, potential allies and vacillating or vulnerable progressive elements. Though Eboe Hutchful (1991: 185) was reflecting generally on Africa, what he scribbles on the use of militarism and constitutionalism to reconstruct political space fits well the Nigerian bill:

"... the overriding political objective has been State preservation and the reconstruction or reinforcement of modes of political dominance. The intention

is less the liberation of national politics than to limit the space of politicseither as a form of activity or as a structural level within the social formation".

Babangida extensive patronage system

Here, we encounter vintage Babangida, seeking to dominate at once his entourage and the totality of his environment. Shortly after he burst into the country's highest political consciousness, the signals came almost in rapid succession that the General knew what he wanted to do in power and with power. He was the first military ruler to declare himself president to the consternation of his colleagues on the Armed Forces Ruling Council (AFRC); he was also the first to dismiss his deputy, Commander Ebitu Ukiwe, well- respected in military circles, and personally invited by the General to be his number two; he was equally the first to dissolve and recompose, at his whims and fancies, the military 'legislative' council. Hence, the eminently sensible claim by Robin Luckham (1994: 43) that, like Acheampong in Ghana and Amin in Uganda, Babangida "took personal control of both army and State from the beginning". But this has to be demonstrated.

There is little doubt that Babangida inherited, like Buhari before him, a political economy that was at once unviable and unenviable. The economic profligacy and massive corruption of the second republic politicians - particularly the Federal Government under the Presidency of Shehu Shagari of the National Party of Nigeria (NPN) - had created a veritable crisis for the continued financial and economic well-being of the country. At the time the Saint-Sylvester (December 31) coup of 1983 was staged, the country already had a high debt profile as well as an important fall in real terms of federal government oil and other receipts (for details see Amuwo, 1988).

The preferred strategy of Buhari to deal with the crisis was counter-trade and rapid debt-servicing. The latter implied strict discipline and immense sacrifice from all Nigerians, including the new junta. The regime did not tolerate laxity either and its combat against drug trafficking may have been its greatest undoing. When it fell in August 1985, little was known about its economic 'success' in a short spate of twenty months. Officially, anyway, it was its alleged political dirigisme that was held responsible for its replacement by the Babangida junta.

The latter may have had an initial sincere commitment to revamping the economy from its patent decadence to a fairly well- functioning proto-capitalist system. A well-orchestrated building- block to this policy option was to allow a nation-wide debate on the desirability of taking an IMF loan. Nigerians did not disappoint Babangida: they overwhelmingly rejected any form of externally-imposed solution to the economic crisis. In a national broadcast, Babangida accepted their decision but pointed to the consequence of same: a 'home-grown' Structural Adjustment Programme (SAP) that would require lots of sacrifice and belt-tightening from diverse groups, interests, classes and individuals. Unknown to the people, Babangida merely got what he bargained for - a *carte blanche* and leeway to reorganize the political economy as he deemed fit.

An IMF-SAP was commenced in June 1986 without the fund's standby facility. Economic efficiency through a combination of fiscal monetary and structural reformation was the overall goal of the policy. Its elements included currency devaluation; subsidy withdrawal (from consumer goods, social welfare and human development services, parastatals, etc.); trade liberalisation and the erection of the market, rather than the State, as king. Certain sectoral implications followed: formal stoppage of import licensing; shrinking of public sector; scrapping marketing boards; privatisation and commercialisation of several public enterprises; deregulation of the financial system.

The foregoing was all fine on paper, but rigour, discipline, investment spirit and other Weberian capitalist ethics were conspicuous by their absence. There was not only a patterned relationship of vacillation between *dirigisme* and *laissez-faire*, there was, worse, a constant breakdown of discipline on the part of the junta. As early as September 1987, "discipline had been lost" (Rimmer, 1994: 105). According to Nils B. Tallroth (in Rimmer) "fiscal policies and control over public expenditure were the most difficult area to implement". The result was fiscal deficits that kept increasing by leaps and bounds. In 1990, 1991 and 1992, these represented, respectively, 12.4%, 9.8% and about 19% of the respective GDP estimates. The 1993 figure was between 15 and 16% of GDP.

Moreover, the 1992 budget deficits represented 48% of total expenditure (Rimmer).

Why this grim picture? Babangida needed a lot of money to run and oil his patron-client network. The money could not have been accounted for to the extent that it was largely outside of the federal revenues and budgetary estimates. But then it had a lot of impact on the latter, resulting, very often, in excess liquidity which the Central Bank would mop up. Ordinary folks were always confounded that whereas government complained of cash crunch for social services and payment of salaries, huge amounts of money were regularly donated by government to sundry manifestations and to government by rich individuals.

Patronage was Babangida's major plank for the pursuit of an inclusive politics and, as we show below, repression, its corollary for groups and individuals that resist political entryism. Like some of his predecessors, the oil industry was perceived as the inexhaustible mine for financing the patronage network. But Babangida had nurtured other business interests before coming to power. They became intensified while in power, with oil providing the unyielding backbone. Like several of his peers - the 'new class' of political generals and propertied serving and retired ex-soldier rulers and senior officers - Babangida had vast interests in construction and real estate (Abacha's privileged domain). The Foundation Mira Construction Company (Abuja) the name of which "does not appear in the corporate registration records in Abuja" and whose senior director, Mustapha Wushishi is Babangida's first cousin *(Africa Confidential,* 22 October 1993) is only one of the many companies in which he had vast interests. There were three others, one of which with initials FN, was nicknamed 'Finish Nigeria' Company by Abuja residents. Towards the end of his reign, Babangida tried his hand on newspapering but the delapitating *Triple Heritage* building, also in Abuja, is a testimony to the failure of that attempt.

The foregoing is nothing compared to Babangida's oil business. Oil may well have been his second love. His claims to nationalism and altruism all fell in one fell swoop by virtue of intricate business ties with sundry foreign interests at the expense of the nation's oil development and the well-being of the people. The General ran the oil industry like a personal fief, granting oil-lifting rights in flagrant violation of stipulated procedures. Indeed, oil ministers rose and fell from grace to grass according to their attitude to this personalization phenomenon. Under him, Marc Rich's Swiss-based

Glencore Company was the most in view in getting short-term oil-lifting contracts.

The latter accounted for no fewer than 50% of the country's total production. An official of the company was quoted as boasting that "we have got 80% of Nigeria (sic), now we are going for the rest" *(Africa Confidential*, 18 November 1994, p. 8). Abacha has maintained these ties, only to add the Chagouri brothers to the list of privileged oil dealers. Yet, the racketeering of Nigeria's oil industry did not start with Babangida. It was inaugurated by General Gowon. Today, the array of personalities involved in the scramble is bewildering. According to a source:

"...the commercial interests of Nigeria's own oil traders are likely to be decisive, in particular former military rulers Generals Yakubu Gowon and Olusegun Obasanjo; General Abacha's sons Ibrahim and Mohammed; and the owner of First Fuels, Abdul Rahman Abdul Rassaq; all of whom are looking to extend their reach and have the political clout to do so" (Africa Confidential, ibid.).

Through a combination of direct control of the oil industry and an expedient implementation of SAP, Babangida was able to foster "economic windfalls for an array of private sector beneficiaries" (Lewis, 1994: 337). These benefitted from diverse opportunities in non-productive sectors of the economy. The list here is a long one: foreign exchange (forex) speculation and hawking by proxy; privatisation of even profitable government companies, sold off in the main, at give-away prices; agricultural exports; petroleum smuggling and drug trafficking ; a free-for-all banking system; urban real estate, etc. These practices did little to help SAP achieve it stated objectives. The question, of course by advantage of hindsight, is whether SAP as implemented was not mounted basically to bolster the rentier- class and, logically, create an institutional base of support for Babangida's private political project?

Consequently, economic and political reforms were aimed, in practice, to realize the following objectives. One, grant Babangida a large *champ de manoeuvre* to determine his preferred political trajectory. Two, bolster a big, if inefficient, State to consolidate resources in the presidency, which could then be used for patronage and spoils.

There were sufficiently important loopholes and leakages, however, to allow a disparate set of elites to benefit as well as distribute the benefits. This is part of the politics of SAP which as in much of Africa, was subtly played by the regime to mobilize the ruralites, putative beneficiaries of SAP, against the 'dispossessed' and 'frustrated' urbanites. It is a neo-indirect rule system, a *pax britannica* of sorts to divide the people in order to control better human and material resources. But as Yusuf Bangura (1992: 66 ff), has argued, this policy option is not always crowned with success (see also various essays in Bayo Olukoshi (1993). Three, allow the regime the perfect opportunity to use pure and cheap blackmail against reform beneficiaries, who would later be accused of using money to corrupt the electorate by a pre-voting purchase, *en masse*, of voters. A vicious cycle of disqualification of one set of beneficiaries would provoke another until the 'political class' - oldbreed and moneybags in particular - was totally discredited. The Newbreed, Babangida's own foster baby, would be too dependent and fragile to make a go at the presidency. They would naturally ask the General to continue in office until a suitable civilian successor is found. This was, *mutatis mutandis*, the ball game. But as we show below there is always a gap between self-perception and self-reality.

Now, the Babangida patronage network was meant to constitute a formidable national constituency of strategically placed elites. The constituency was to be anchored on his military faction - afterall a military regime's first consideration is security and survival - but with vertical and horizontal tentacles nation-wide. A largely truncated national constituency was created and was made up of two layers. The first layer consisted of a mixed grill of mainly right-wing elements from the various factions and fractions of the national ruling clique - military, political, bureaucratic, intelligentsia, commerco-business, chiefly estates (or Royal Fathers).

The second layer was made up of a hodge-podge of upstarts, from all walks of life. Some of them may have genuinely believed in the regime's 'grassroots' democracy and new political culture and therefore offered themselves for politics and public service. Others may simply have wanted to have a go at rent-seeking and the relatively easy life that it entailed.

The first layer was referred to by the regime as the oldbreed or moneybags who, having been implicated in the corruption of the previous republics, were no longer fit to lead the nation. The Nigerian Press, nicknames them 'Any-Government-in-Power' (AGIP) people. One is always fascinated by their longevity in holding power. They have lived virtually all their lives in the public arena; living off and on the State. Theirs is an indefinite discourse in the composition of a ruling clique. Those of them who fall from grace in one regime have a way of bouncing back in the next.

Precisely because of their experience and good knowledge of the political terrain - with all its class and non-class differentiations or dissimilarities - they are not just beholden to government; the latter is forced, some of the time, to succumb to their pressures and wishes. The point here is that the Babangida network was a two-way traffic of power and resource relations. To be sure, as the sole purveyor and dispenser of largesse, Babangida tended to often dominate proceedings to the extent that the greatest vulnerability of this layer of support system was that it got broken easily. Given the ease with which financial resources are procured it is not surprising that these resources dry up as soon as they are obtained.

This vulnerability would also be a major set-back for progressive, pro-democracy groups and individuals who, under a SAP regime, sometimes found Babangida patronage, in whatever form, irresistible. Indeed, the General perfected the act of what came to be known as the politics of settlement, namely "timely doses of cash to anesthetize the opposition and buy off labour unions and other powerful grumblers" (Peter da Costa, 1993: 53-57). The aim was always to implicate as many social groups as possible in the corruption of the network in order to render them politically impotent thereafter. For all of the seeming subservience of the oldbreed and moneybags to Babangida, they were never fully trusted.

Not only did he keep a tab, in particular, on the commercial-business elites, in order to temper their resistance and antagonism, occasionally publicly vented (Lewis, 1994: 337), but the entire network was a thick layer of surveillance and counter-surveillance. Babangida himself had a solid reputation for being an active nocturnal worker. He spent much time on the phone, particularly after the gubernatorial elections in December 1991, solicitous after reluctant politicians to join the race for the Presidency and the Senate (8), the House of Representatives having been reserved for 'his' newbreed politicians, many of whom he personally sponsored.

Each presidential aspirant that got personal phone calls and letters of support from Babangida kept the information close to his chest supposing he was the favoured candidate. The controversial cancellation of the presidential primaries of the two political parties, the Social Democratic Party (SDP) and the National Republican Convention (NRC) in October 1992 - after retired General Yar'Adua had won the SDP ticket and Adamu Ciroma and Umaru Shinkafi were set for a run-off for the NRC ticket - was the first eye-opener. The last two politicians and Bamanga Tukur, who ran a close third, discovered, to their chagrin, that Babangida had been sending his agents to each of them urging him on. At a press conference thereafter in Kaduna, the trio declared the military "the greatest obstacle to democracy in Nigeria".

Yet, that lesson was lost on the new set of presidential aspirants including M.K.O. Abiola and Babagana Kingibe. After clinching the SDP ticket in Jos in March 1993, literally at photofinish, it was a herculean task for the party to firm up a running mate for Abiola. Sixty four meetings after, Kingibe, former party chairman and second to Abiola in the primaries, was finally chosen. Each of them went to Babangida for consultations. Abiola who would confess after his presidential mandate was annulled on June 23, 1995, by the regime that he consulted with the highest office in the land before contesting -, was advised to reject Kingibe. The latter was said to be too much of a party man, who could ultimately undermine a future Abiola presidency. Kingibe was also at Aso Rocks where he was advised not to tarry in accepting the Abiola offer.

It would appear that for Babangida and his clients what was most important was the mutual utility of the network. He opened the politico-economic space for his clients to pursue their rent- seeking activities. And rent-seekers are not particularly enamoured by democratic theories and practices because "they will see democratization as a threat to their livelihood" (John M. Mbaku, 1994: 283). Since one good turn deserves another, Babangida's clients would later provide the necessary foot troops to bring succour to their patron and help massage his deflated ego just before he hurriedly 'stepped aside' on August 26, 1993.

There was yet another modality in keeping clients happy and busy: creation of more States and local governments, even at inauspicious moments was meant to widen networks of patronage to new State and local government elites and to delay return to civil rule for as long as possible. To be sure, persistent fractionalization of Nigeria under Babangida tended to reinforce the centrality and criticality of the federal government. In a fundamental sense, Babangida exploited this "centralized configuration of State power to impose his own whimsical vision on Nigeria" (Tunji Lardner jr, 1990: 51).

The Politics of Repression

The rationale for the politics of repression, by which I mean the curbing of associational life and the dwarfing of the civic public realm within the context of the transition programme, was furnished by SAP. Bangura (1992: 73) offers a sophisticated interpretation of democratization by the Babangida regime with SAP: democratization would appear to be a strategy to regulate the anticipated popular opposition to the economic reform programme. In this regard the military wields considerable authority in determining the evolution of the transition plan.

Whilst the foregoing was clearly a class project, it was more of the workings of a pathological crave for personal power. As usual, the issue was presented in corporatist terms; non-State actors were routinely accused of sabotaging the impeding new order and the hand-over plans. The political alibi used until after the annulment was that the regime would not hand-over in chaos. I will rapidly examine two levels of analysis here.

Scenarios of Failure

This is a more subtle form of political repression. Yet, it is a no-win situation. As summarized by Luckham (1994: 64), "military rulers like Babangida... in Nigeria... have placed obstacles in the way of democratic openings at every turn" (see also Amuwo, 1990; Agbese and Kieh, 1992; Rotimi and Ihonvbere, 1994; D. Bach, 1995 (a) and (b)). From the outset, the regime made it clear that the transition programme was sacrosanct; it was a top-down 'liberalisaton' process, the timing and contents of which only the regime could decide. Yet, each phase lent itself to severe contestation on account of several inconsistencies and much panel beating and fine-tuning. Similarly, high political and electoral standards that could not possibly have been met by any mortal (e.g. volume of registration papers by the political associations that would later be outlawed in October 1989) were set ostensibly to discredit the political class in the eyes of the public.

It was, in this respect, very curious that the regime did little to protect Newbreed politicians who had been presented, as already pointed out, as the torch-bearers of 'a new socio-political order'. By 1993, a close observer of the transition concluded that Babangida wanted an indefinite stay in power. Written in a rather gadfly and condescending tone, Lewis (1994: 131-133) noted: "The evolution of events during the final years of the transition process led many observers to conclude that Babangida never had any real intention relinquishing power to civilians".

He provided evidence: while NEC was a "modicum of proficiency", because under Professor Humphrey Nwosu, it "functioned with diligence and integrity as an overseer of the electoral system', nonetheless it was "continually subject to the dictates of the Babangida regime and was largely relegated to implementing military stipulations".

The political class was another proof. For Lewis, under Babangida, the politicians were "more reliant on the magnanimity of the generals, as the president intermittently recertified and reshuffled the political elite according to whim".

Attempt at Incapacitation of Non-State Actors

Military regimes seek, almost by definition, a monopoly of the public and political space in order to complement and reinforce their monopoly of coercive apparati of the State. This objective is not always pursued by exclusively violent modalities, however. As we have shown, there is a selective use of patronage - they are generous to groups and individuals adjudged to have 'correct' political behaviour; but very stringent and miserly vis-a-vis perceived opposition groups. More often than not, patronage is a form of moral pressure to make them fall in line. The two modalities - repression and patronage, stick and carrot - are meant to undermine collective consciousness of associations and individuals opposed to a commandist approach to civil governance (R. Mustapha, 1992: 214).

In Nigeria, the country's rich pluralistic political economy often poses a serious obstacle to this search for double hegemony. It was in his confrontation with non-State actors that Babangida was at his negative best. But it was on that terrain, too, that he was politically worsted.

CHAPTER THIRTEEN
IBB and the OIC

It was under him that Nigeria joined the Organization of Islamic countries and was pumping money into that Arab owned political/economic group. While his minions were declaring Islamic legal code in their states across the North, in the 1985-1993 that he was military president, Nigeria became an Islamic state. His second in command, Navy Commodore Ebitu Ukiwe was removed from being in that office for being bold enough to tell journalists that the issue of Nigeria being in the OIC was never discussed in Federal Executive meetings. The sultanate demanded his removal for being so bold to challenge their position.

Babangida was so single minded, self-centered, and power-drunk, he single-handedly forced OIC membership on Nigeria without respect for our supposed religious secularity. He used every means imaginable to assert his power. Spiritual, criminal, everything was fair in his ruthless power game. The gods of the Marabouts became privileged guests at Aso Rock, lacing it with severe witchcraft, which was later vigorously sustained by Abacha.

CHAPTER FOURTEEN
Oputa report indicts IBB, just like the Okigbo report

NON APPEARANCE OF THE THREE GENERALS

It became clear to us that the issue of the appearance or otherwise of the former Heads State was a matter of national significance. For the sake of the records, it is important to refresh the minds of all Nigerians on the initiatives which the Commission took which culminated in the decision to issue a Composite Ruling on October 3, 2001. The Commission went to great lengths to explain to our former leaders that they had a legal, moral and even political duty to honour the call of Nigerians and that the issues were not merely between them and the Commission. We explained that the summons was in reality the voice of Nigerians who were simply interested in knowing as much about the events in their country as possible.

The legal dimension of the cases was addressed by the three learned gentlemen who represented the former Heads of State and other interested respected lawyers. The key issue here was that of the appearances of the former Heads of State who had defied the Commission but still wished to first appear through their lawyers, and then secondly have their lawyers cross examine the witnesses. The Commission decided to listen to various opinions before arriving at its decision. Those who addressed this very lively session of the Commission on the legal issues were:

- Chief G.O. K Ajayi, SAN
- Chief Clement Akpambgo, SAN
- Chief Shola Rhodes, SAN
- Chief Olajide Ayodele, SAN
- Mr. Emmanuel Toro, SAN
- Chief Gani Fawehinmi, SAN

There were three issues for determination. They were:

i.   Whether the Commission, relying on Section 5 of the Tribunals of Inquiry Act, Cap 447 had the vires or the Constitutional competence to issue and serve witness summonses or the former Heads of State.

ii.   Whether the former Heads of State can appear by proxy, i.e. through their lawyers, assuming that (i) above is not ultra vires?

iii.   Whether, having disobeyed the summonses of the Commission to appear in person to testify, they can be allowed to cross examine other witnesses for the Commission?

The Commission reviewed the evidence submitted before it and concluded that there was really only one central question which was: Do proceedings before a Commission of Inquiry constitute a suit at law or a judicial proceeding? In its wisdom, the Commission came to the conclusion that: In a Commission of Inquiry under the Act, there does not exist an adversary situation. There is no litigation, and as such, there are no parties properly so called. No judgment is entered or can be even entered for or against the parties that do not in law exist. Everyone who appears before the Commission appears as a witness whose evidence will enable the Commission gather all the facts and make recommendations to the Proper Authority contemplated in Section 14 of the Act.... From our Terms of Reference, every President or ex-President, every top government functionary from January 15th, 1966 to May 28th 1999 is a relevant and necessary witness, whether or not he is specifically mentioned or implicated in any petition before the Commission.

It is therefore no defence for failure to attend to say that any particular official was not mentioned in any particular petition. It is also erroneous to suggest that questions ought to be limited to the averments in a particular petition... That being so, every Head of State during those dark military years will be held accountable. He has to give account to the people of Nigeria, give account of his stewardship in respect of all gross human rights violations committed during his period of office. He is also accountable to history.

The Commission, in its ruling went to great lengths to acquaint the two presidents with the fact that it was wrong for them to even speculate that they were being singled out for persecution since even the serving President had been issued with a summons. What is more, the Commission pointed out that it was not just a question of serving as Head of state that warranted their being summoned. Two former Heads of State, Alhaji Shehu Shagari and Chief Ernest Shonekan, were not summoned because no petitions were pending against them, nor were they in any way mentioned in any pending petition.

On whether it could exercise its powers of section, the Commission again, in its Composite ruling argued that although Section 10 of the Act empowers the Commission to issue a warrant of arrest to any person failing to attend on summons, it believed that: discretion is usually the better part of valour. The Commission, it ruled, is on a reconciliation process and one does not reconcile under duress.... The failure or refusal of our former Heads of State to attend has rudely shaken the faith and confidence of Nigerians in the reconciliation process Military rule thrives on the culture of impunity, which means that the leaders are both above the law and beyond punishment. Impunity, which is what the refusal to attend portrays, destroys the confidence of the people in the authority and role of the State. Since they did not avail themselves of the opportunity to come and tell their own side of the story, as the President and some former and serving senior governments functionaries did, we leave a blank space on our records against each and everyone of the three former Heads of State as evidence that we are leaving them and their side of the story in the court of human history.

We recommend to the Federal Government that all the former Heads of state be considered to have surrendered their right to govern Nigeria and Nigerians at any other time in the future. It is left for Nigerians to judge.

The Commission also wishes to state as follows:

i. On General Muhammad Buhari, the Commission is of the view that the General has a case to answer in regard to the killing of the three young men referred to in the petition brought by the Kenneth Owoh family. There was overwhelming evidence to show that the execution of the three young men fell well outside the time frame allowed by the Decree under which they were tried. We therefore recommend that the General tender an unreserved apology to the families of the deceased. We equally hold accountable the Supreme Military Council of General Muhammadu Buhari that confirmed the brutal execution of the three young men. We therefore hold the then Supreme Military Council accountable.

On General Ibrahim Babangida, we are of the view that there is evidence to suggest that he and the two security chiefs, Brigadier General Halilu Akilu and Col. A. K. Togun are accountable for the death of Dele Giwa by letter bomb. We recommend that this case be re-open for further investigation in the public interest.

On the government of General Abdusalami Abubakar, the case against him had already been well argued by one of the witnesses, Col Idenhere, who testified in the case. Although he was not directly mentioned in the death of Chief Abiola, the inconsistency in the testimony of his Chief Security Officer, Lt Col Aliyu show that the Government of the day knows much more about the circumstances leading to the death of the chief. We therefore recommend that that government is accountable.By refusing to appear before the Commission, they denied themselves the wonderful opportunity of explaining to Nigerians what happened in each case, like General T. Y. Danjuma and Dr. Walter Ofonagoro did.

CHAPTER FOURTEEN
IBB and Okigbo's report

He stole more than $12 billion dollars from the oil windfall that Nigeria enjoyed at the desert storm of 1991 when the United States first invaded Iraq to drive Sadam out of Kuwait.

Babangida is also known to be part of the group of past heads of states of Nigeria that got bribed by Halliburton of the United States. Though the Federal government has refused to make public the report, which made it difficult for any one to publish, parts of its content was however revealed in a well publicized report on various newspapers in Nigeria.

Here is an excerpt from the Punch newspaper;

Former Military President, Gen. Ibrahim Babangida, frittered away $12bn of the country's revenue through special accounts, which he ran as the sole approving authority.

This was contained in the report of the Panel on the Reorganisation and Reforms of the Central Bank of Nigeria. The panel headed by the late renowned economist, Dr. Pius Okigbo, painted in graphic details how Babangida operated "a second but undisclosed budget" with the then CBN governor, the late Alhaji Abdulkadir Ahmed. The report, which was submitted to the administration of the late Gen. Sani Abacha on August 29, 1994, had been a subject of interest to Nigerians, who have been itching for the detailed report of the government's White Paper on it.

According to the report, the Babangida regime operated dedication accounts outside of the budgetary provisions, which he ran without accounting to anybody. It stated that the operations of these accounts were fraught with irregularities. "The proceeds of the sale of the crude were not shown in the revenue side nor were the expenditures reflected in the expenditure side of the budget," the report said.

The report traced the origin of the accounts to September 1988 when Babangida approved a proposal to dedicate 65,000 barrels of crude oil per day for certain priority projects, particularly the Ajaokuta Steel, the Itakpe Iron Mining and the Shiroro Hydroelectric projects. It added that the quantity was increased to 105,000bpd in October 1989 to finance such projects as the LNG and the commitment to the Joint Venture Partners of the Nigerian National Petroleum Corporation. In the early part of 1994, it was again raised to 150,000bpd.

The report disclosed that the "total receipts and payments in respect of the dedication accounts from inception in September 1988 to June 30, 1994 were $6.195bn and $6.109bn respectively, leaving a balance of $85.943m as at the end of the period." Other controversial special accounts allegedly opened by the then military regime, according to the report, included the NNPC Sales of Mining Account, the Stabilisation Account, the Signature Bonus Account, and the GHQ Special Fund Account.

While the $2.06bn accrued to the NNPC Sales of Mining Rights Account, through the sale of mining rights in the NNPC/ Shell Joint venture, $4.398bn accrued to the Stabilisation Account between October 1990 and June, 1994. As the report explained, the Stabilisation Account was created in October 1990 to receive revenue from crude oil sales in excess of the budgeted provision during the Gulf War.

The aim, it added, was to effectively separate it from the Federation Account and to sterilise it pending instructions for further utilisation. It reported that the bulk of the money was applied to settle obligations outstanding to contractors handling priority projects and in financing the debt buy-back operation.

The report further disclosed that in 1992 $1.21bn, representing the proceeds of debt held by the CBN was received back into the account, but the balance in that account as June 30, 1994 was $117.36m. There was no account of the disbursements from that account. The report added that as the funds swelled, other revenue streams, including the proceeds from the sale of mining rights, stabilisation accounts, and signature bonus, were also squandered.

The Babangida regime, it said, also resorted to the financing of mundane projects like the purchase of television and video sets for the Presidency at the cost of $18.30m, documentary film on Nigeria, $2.92m, and foreign trips by wife of the President, $8.95m, and medical clinic for Aso Rock, $27.25m, among others. It said, "Neither the Dedication Account nor the Stabilisation Account was applied for the .purpose it was originally designed to serve. "Thus, the Dedication Account was used for many non-priority projects and the Stabilisation Account was not, in practice, used to sterilise revenues in excess of projected earnings". "Instead, after a short delay, the monies in the accounts were spent virtually as fast as they were accumulated."

On the external sector of the economy, the report insisted that there was nothing to cheer about the various economic policies employed by the Babangida administration in the reviewed period. "It noted that in spite of the various policy measures and put in place since 1986 to reverse the deteriorating trend in the external sector of the economy, the results were unsatisfactory". "The noticeable favourable performance in the balance of payments in the first year of the implementation of the Structural Adjustment Programme, 1986-1988, was artificial as some debt service claims against the country were postponed due to debt rescheduling." It argued that the improvement could have been sustained but for the usually high level of other external payments and expenditures from 1989 onwards, which wiped out the external reserves and put extreme pressures on the balance of payments.

It noted that the external sector performance deteriorated in 1992 as the overall balance of payments position, which was persistently in surplus during the previous three years, plunged into huge deficit of $3.8bn. This, according to the report, reflected the large payments made in respect of scheduled amortisation, as well as the debt buy-back arrangement, which led to the repurchase of $3.4bn worth of the country's external debt.

Other members of the panel were the incumbent Chairman, First Bank of Nigeria Plc, Alhaji Umaru Mutallab; the current Chairman of Diamond Bank, Mr. Paschal Dozie; Mr. Y. Sankey; and Mrs. B. Latinwo. Others were the current Secretary to the Government of the Federation, Chief Ufot Ekaette; Mr. O. Oyefodunrin; and Ida, who was the secretary.
Efforts to find out the present state of the various accounts listed in the report from the CBN met a brick wall.

The bank's Head of Corporate Affairs, Mr. Festus Odoko, said in a telephone interview on Monday that he could not say much on the issue since the Federal Government had not released the report to the public. When pressed further, the CBN spokesman who requested for a copy of the report dismissed the claims that certain spurious accounts were managed by the CBN. "I do not know anywhere in the world where CBN opens account for individuals. There are accounts for banks and government," Odoko said.

In an interview with THISDAY on Sunday, on August 20, 2006, Babangida said he had anticipated the oil windfall as one of the major political issues against his presidential aspiration in 2007. He, however, added that he was prepared to defend the management of the $12.4bn. He said, "I prepared my mind. I knew what everybody will be talking about. Now, they have added Vatsa into the vocabulary of the atrocities committed by IBB. "So, it's Vatsa, the N12.4bn oil windfall they say I stole; Dele Giwa; June 12 and the institutionalisation of corruption. I hope Nigerians will believe (and I believe they will) when we eventually tell them the truth. "I said for my eight years, I have never been so fortunate to get a barrel of crude oil above $30. I was that unfortunate to manage a situation where a barrel sold for $12, $10 per barrel during my regime. On one side, you had me who managed poverty, on the other side; you had others who are managing affluence."

The Coordinator, International Press Centre, Lagos, Mr. Lanre Arogundade, on Monday said the failure by the government to make the report public and issue a White Paper on it raised a major question mark on the genuineness of its anti-corruption war. Also, the Executive Director, Media Rights Agenda, Mr. Edaetan Ojo, said he was surprised by the government's lack of commitment to get to the root of the case despite the amount of money involved and its anti-corruption stance. They spoke on Monday in separate interviews with our correspondents.

While commending THE PUNCH for its efforts at putting the report in the public domain, Ojo said his organisation would take the issue up once it had the necessary tools.
Despite the fact that THE PUNCH had it on good authority that a copy of the report had been with Ida, past attempts to get it were unsuccessful.

On October 13, 2004, THE PUNCH wrote Ekaette, asking for the government's intervention to obtain the report. But the letter was not replied. A reminder, signed by the Editor, THE PUNCH, Mr. Azubuike Ishiekwene, was sent to the SGF on October 27. The SGF, whose office statutorily keeps all reports of panels or commissions of inquiry, sent a terse response on November 12, 2004.

In the response, signed by Dr. K.B. Kaigama on behalf of the SGF, the government said it would be willing to make the Okigbo Report available as soon as it could be found. Still unrelenting, THE PUNCH, on April 11, 2005, wrote a letter to the chairman of the defunct National Political Reform Conference, Justice Niki Tobi, urging the conference to prevail on the government to release the reports of both the Okigbo Panel and the Human Rights Violations and Investigations Commission to the public. The NPRC did not address the issues bordering on the Okigbo Report.

Having obtained a copy of the report, THE PUNCH on August 10, 2006, wrote another letter to the SGF to verify its authenticity and enclosed the 352-page report. Extracts from the letter read, "You may recall, Sir, that on October 13 and 27, 2004, PUNCH wrote two separate letters to the SGF requesting for copies of the Okigbo panel report, which among other things, investigated how the military administration of General Ibrahim Babangida disbursed the $12.4bn earned from the sale of oil during the first Gulf War in 1990/1991.

"PUNCH was also encouraged to write because the present administration had indicated quite clearly, both in public comments by President Olusegun Obasanjo and specifically in a reply to our enquiries in a letter received on Friday, November 12, 2004 (signed by Dr. K.B. Kaigama on behalf of the SGF), that it would be willing to make the Okigbo report available as soon as it can be found. "In fact, we recall that as part of the government's effort to address our request, Kaigama said in his letter that the SGF's office had written one Alhaji Ibrahim Ida, a member of the panel, for a copy of the report and that his response was being awaited. "After years of diligent search, PUNCH has obtained what could be a genuine copy of the Okigbo report. We would be most obliged if the SGF, who on page VI of the report is indicated as one of the eight members of the panel, and a signatory, could assist PUNCH in verifying the authenticity of this volume in the overriding interest of the public." As at press time on Monday, there was no response or acknowledgement from the government.

CHAPTER FIFTEEN
IBB and public outcry

It is important to take a look at some of the headlines making the news concerning the declaration of General Babangida ambition for the presidency comes 2011.

Some of the materials have been abridged to create enough space but without distortion to the element of truth and facts.

APPENDIX I

$12.4bn oil windfall: Babangida has a case to answer, says Falana

Following a petition by a coalition of civil society groups in the country seeking accountability for the missing $12.4 oil windfall, former military president General Ibrahim Gbadamosi Babangida (rtd) has reportedly said that he "was not indicted by the Okigbo Report", and that much of the funds were concentrated on infrastructural development of the Federal Capital Territory, Abuja. Well, these claims fly in the face of the clear and unambiguous conclusions of the Okigbo report. Let us be very clear about what the report said. The Okigbo report made several conclusions about the missing $12.4bn but I will highlight here just a few. First, the report said that "the approved budget for the Federation did not reflect the receipts into the Dedication and other Special Accounts; that the balances kept in these accounts were not included in the Federation Account, a practice which violated the fundamental precepts of the federal fiscal relations in Nigeria, and that in a number of cases, there were significant variations between the amounts approved for payment and the actual disbursements made, without any further explanation from the documents supplied."

Second, the report said that "in a large number of cases, there were no indications, in the letters written to the Head of State seeking approval to make payments or seeking ex-post approval, as to which dedication account was to be charged - either Dedication, Sale of Mining Rights, Signature Bonus, or Stabilisation Accounts. In such cases, it would be impossible to ascertain, on the basis of the information available, whether or not the approvals were in respect of any of these special accounts. And yet it was the Governor of Central Bank who instructed as to which particular account was to be debited. The Central Bank was never able to establish that payments on behalf of the Ministry of Defence and the National intelligence Agency were based on genuine and well established contracts or transactions. This was because the relevant documents were never made available to the Bank; as such documents were regarded as classified items."

Third, the report stated that, "The funds accruing to these accounts had been applied mainly to payments for services of contractors, and for the purchase of military equipment and services. The gross takings on these accounts from their inception in 1988 to June 1994 totalled $12.4billion. These had been held totally outside the country s external reserves. Indeed, if the funds had been counted as part of the external reserves and had been held as such, the impact on the exchange rate in time years under review would have been so significant that the Naira would have been stronger in 1994, in relation to the dollar, than it was in 1985 when it stood at N1 to $1.004. It should be evident, therefore, that the burden of external debt to the Paris and London Clubs and the pressure on the exchange rate would have been substantially mitigated if not completely eliminated. It is this fact that calls to question the wisdom and prudence not in the creation of these accounts but in its disbursements."

According to the report, "the operation of such accounts was not subject to the normal budgetary processes, and therefore lacked transparency. By limiting the authorisation process for its operation to the approval of the President or Head of State, which was communicated directly only to the CBN Governor, it created considerable room for abuse of procedures, abuse of application and reduced accountability".

Also, there is no single reference in the report to back the claim that the funds were spent to develop the Federal Capital Territory, Abuja. In fact, the funds for Abuja were contained in the Federation Account. As the Okigbo report stated, "there were many large projects of doubtful viability and many more of clearly misplaced priority. In addition to these, the Dedication and Special Accounts had become a parallel budget for the Presidency. The decision as to what expenditure items to be financed out of these dedicated accounts was made by the President alone. For example, the accounts had been utilised to defray aim assortment of expenses that could not in any way be described as priority such as: $2.92 million to make Documentary Film on Nigeria; $18.30 million to purchase TV/Video for the Presidency; $23.98 million for Staff Welfare in the Presidency; $99 million for travels of the First Lady abroad; and $59.72 million for security."

Therefore, it is clear that no indictment can be greater than the above direct conclusions and quotations from the report. The point is that Nigerians deserve explanations as to what exactly happened to the accrued oil revenue of $12.4bn which apparently went missing during the Babangida government. And anyone who loves this country would expect accountability for the missing funds. No amount of misinformation or misrepresentation of the facts and conclusions of the Okigbo report by anyone can stop the demand by Nigerians for accountability in this matter. The action by the civil society groups is indeed patriotic.

APPENDIX II

Return Of The Evil Genius

Babajide Kolade-Otitoju, The News

General Ibrahim Badamasi Babangida (rtd) and Ogun State governor, Otunba Gbenga Daniel, have a few things in common. Both men are fiercely ambitious, self-regarding and seek to dominate every space. They both harbour undisguised desires to play a big role in the post-Yar'Adua era. They are also generous with smiles. In the last few years, because both men have discovered their similarities, their friendship has grown in leaps and bounds. In May 2008, Babangida visited Sagamu, Ogun State. His mission was to commiserate with Daniel over the death of his mother. Daniel also used the visit to get Babangida to settle the rift between him and the state House of Assembly members, which had led to the impeachment of the speaker, Titi Oseni and her deputy, Ayo Odugbesan.

In Sagamu, Daniel and Babangida traded lavish praise. The wily old fox said Daniel had the qualities to play "a greater role in the future of Nigeria", adding that he was visiting Sagamu because of the great respect he had for Daniel, whom he described as "an exemplary achiever". Daniel "retaliated" by describing the man who annulled Nigeria's freest and verifiably fairest election as "a great man who has been able to keep his friends in and out of power". "Previously, I had been a distant admirer of the IBB phenomenon but recently, I have been a great admirer," the governor gushed. On that day, even the Awujale of Ijebuland, Oba Sikiru Adetona, aware of the huge baggage that Babangida carries over his annulment of the 1993 presidential election, pleaded that IBB be forgiven for this indiscretion.

It is intriguing that Babangida chose the occasion of Daniel's pre-birthday lecture held on Thursday 1 April to drop the hint that he could contest the presidency in 2011, and that he was making consultations with a view to disclosing his ambition. While thanking his guests, Daniel appealed to Nigerians to forgive Babangida for whatever mistakes he might have made. "While we may fault some of his actions and inaction, while holding the reins of power of our country, his passion for the progress and peace of Nigeria can hardly be faulted. Yet, his errors of judgement at one point or the other, I am convinced, are not unforgivable," he said.

Then on 10 April, inside the Unity Hall of Government House, Asaba, Babangida officially declared his intention to run for presidency. He was the chief guest of honour at the memorial lecture in honour of his wife, Maryam. Among those present at the event were Governor Aliyu Babangida of Niger State, Ekiti State deputy governor, Sikiru Lawal; and Governor Peter Obi of Anambra State. At the palace of the Asagba of Asaba, Professor Chika Edozien, Babangida picked the traditional title of Dike Doziani, his 68th. The Asagba declared: "It is evident, from the events of our past that our country is in need of you. We hope that you will not hesitate to make it possible for us all to benefit in full from your experience, leadership, wisdom and popularity."

Sources close to Babangida told TheNEWS last week that the former military president, who was forced to step aside on 27 August 1993, has always believed that he will return to Aso Rock someday. His decision in 1998 to back Olusegun Obasanjo in the 1999 presidential election was because he thought Obasanjo would return the favour after Obasanjo must have exhausted his second term in office. As it turned out, Obasanjo refused to return the compliment. Shortly after Babangida picked up the nomination form of the Peoples Democratic Party, PDP, Obasanjo held a meeting with him, where he told him pointedly that he will not back him and that Babangida should join him to pick a younger candidate.

"What many Nigerians did not realise was that after Babangida suffered that setback late in 2006 he never gave up. He never gives up. He bides his time and waits for another day. He has spent the past four years planning how to take another shot at the presidency. He sees this as the right time to move and the question is not whether IBB will contest. It is whether anybody in today's Nigeria can stop him," declared one of Babangida's loyalists who spoke with TheNEWS. This magazine was told that he indeed has acquired sufficient arsenal to wage a political battle. He has reportedly made sorties across political divides and he is convinced that he stands a good chance this time. Critics believe that the boldness displayed by IBB could have to do with his massive war chest. But he said on British Broadcasting Corporation, BBC's Focus on Africa programme that he would not buy his way into office 17 years after leaving the seat of power.

Then on the allegation of corruption against him, IBB acknowledged the fact that he is "the most investigated Nigerian living today". He argued that if he were such a thief, he would have been caught. As he put it: "perhaps after 17 years, it ought to have come out by now (results of probes), unless somebody is not doing his job". He also reacted to the most vexed political issue in the last decade- annulment of June 12 1993 election. IBB claimed that he organised the freest and fairest election ever but that "the fact that it was annulled is a difficult story altogether".

Babangida's declaration of intent to contest the presidency in 2011 has kicked up public anger. Pastor Tunde Bakare of the Latter Rain Assembly and convener of the Save Nigeria Group, SNG, called on Nigerians to pelt Babangida with stones whenever he declares his interest to contest. Bakare described Babangida as a clever manipulator and an arrogant megalomaniac who has refused to apologise for the annulment of the 1993 presidential election believed to have been won by Chief M.K.O. Abiola. He added that though the former military president has the right to vie for an elective office, he should not because he messed the country up when he was in power and so does not have anything new to offer Nigerians. "Let's vote for IBB with stones. Make sure the stones have rough edges," he said.

Similarly, Professor Itse Sagay, a constitutional lawyer, described IBB's ambition as an insult to Nigerians. He blamed IBB for institutionalising corruption in Nigeria at a time when General Muhammadu Buhari (retd) was about abolishing it. "He scuttled our democracy and ushered in the Abacha era fraught with gross human rights abuse. It will never happen for IBB to contest election in this country," Sagay said. Reverend Ola Makinde, Prelate of the Methodist Church, was more critical in his assessment of IBB's ambition. He believes that Babangida owes Nigerians an explanation, particularly on the death of Dele Giwa. "We don't want a religious bigot to rule us. He introduced the nation to the Organisation of Islamic Conference, OIC. He has to explain to us why. We have lost so many souls and properties worth billions of naira. He has to explain the disappearance of the oil windfall," Makinde said.

Chief Reuben Fasoranti, an Afenifere chieftain, wonders what Babangida wants from Nigeria and urged him to forget about the presidency. "He should allow fresh blood to move into the polity," he said. Segun Gbadegesin, writing in his column in the 9 April edition of The NATION, noted that Babangida's presidential ambition is meant to redeem his battered image. This, to him, is an uphill task. "Babangida should know that he cannot redeem himself with another presidential round," he wrote. Gbadegesin reckoned that it is only in Africa and Nigeria in particular, that politicians are not satisfied with eight or more years in government. "They want to have more or die in office. If the experience of others is anything to go by, he may even come out worse," he said.

But Babangida also has sympathisers. Ahmad Muhammad, a columnist, is one of them. Writing in the 10 April edition of ThisDay, Muhammad reasoned that IBB is a seasoned and astute administrator, who has the best interest of Nigeria at heart. "He is fair, competent, honest and achievement-driven, and has done more to advance the cause of democracy than most politicians, despite his military background. In my opinion, Babangida has been more democratic than any other Nigerian leader since 1966," he said. Muhammad, who was reacting to "Why I won't Vote for the Generals", an opinion in the 3 April edition of the same paper, written by Dele Momodu, publisher of Ovation magazine, struggled frantically to bail IBB out of the questions posed to the former dictator.

On why IBB is still interested in the presidency even at almost 70, Muhammad claimed Babangida is a young man. "In this 21st century, Babangida is, by modern definition, a middle-aged man because the criteria for classifying people have changed," he said. On why Babangida is often linked with the murder of Dele Giwa, Muhammad inferred that IBB became the suspect simply because he was then the head of state. He argued further that if such great lawyers like the late Chief Gani Fawehinmi failed to find credible evidence against IBB, the reason must be that they were looking in the wrong direction.

On the annulment of the election, Muhammed defended Babangida thus: "He (Momodu) should remember that Abiola was IBB's best friend. My take is that IBB was pained, and still probably is, by the annulment. Babangida has himself stated that he would explain the annulment at the appropriate time." Muhammad added that in the event that Babangida is reluctant to contest the 2011 presidential election, he would rally Nigerians to coerce him to join the race. He concluded that the country badly needs a natural and truly democratic leader, which IBB represents. "We should urge him to come to the rescue. I suspect that even Dele Momodu will vote for him," he concluded.

Similarly, Godwin Daboh, president of Benue State Elders' Forum and a PDP chieftain, thinks the country cannot produce a leader better than Babangida. To him, Babangida is the best thing that has, and will ever happen to Nigeria. As far as a coalition of Nigeria's civil society groups is concerned, Babangida remains indicted over the reckless spending of the $12.4 billion Gulf War oil windfall. Babangida recently declared through his media aide, Kassim Afegbua, that he was not indicted by the Pius Okigbo report on the missing $12.4b, and that the bulk of the money was spent on infrastructural development of the Federal Capital Territory, Abuja.

Last week, Femi Falana, President, West African Bar Association, WABA, told TheNEWS that there are unambiguous conclusions of the Okigbo report, which indicted the gap-toothed general. "First, the report said the approved budget for the federation did not reflect the receipts into the dedicated and other special accounts, that the balances kept in these accounts were not included in the federal account, a practice which violated the fundamental precepts of the federal fiscal relations in Nigeria, and that in a number of cases, there were significant variations between amounts approved for payment and the actual disbursements made, without further explanation from the documents supplied," Falana argued.

He affirmed that, according to the Okigbo Report, in large number of cases, "There were not indications in the letters written to the head of state seeking approval to make payments or seeking express approval as to which dedicated account was to be charged, either dedicated, sales or mining rights, signature bonus or stabilisation accounts. In such cases it will be impossible on the basis of information available [to determine] whether or not the approvals were in respect of any of these special accounts."

Indeed, according to the Okigbo Report, "the Central Bank of Nigeria was not able to establish that payments on behalf of the Ministry of Defence and the National Intelligence Agency were based on genuine and well established contracts or transactions." The report says: "The operation of the accounts was not subject to the normal budgetary processes and therefore lacked transparency," adding that there were many large projects of doubtful viability and many more of clearly misplaced priority.

According to the report, the Dedicated and Special Accounts had become a parallel budget for the presidency, with the decision as to what expenditure items to be financed out of these dedicated accounts made by president alone. The report listed expenses which could not be described as priority such as $2.92million to make documentary film on Nigeria, $18.30 million to purchase TV/Video for the presidency, $23.98 million for staff welfare in the presidency, $99 million for travels of the first lady abroad and $59.72 million for security. In the opinion of Falana, no indictment can be greater than these conclusions from the Okigbo Report. He noted that Nigerians deserved explanation as to what happened to the accrued oil revenue of $12.4bn, which went missing during the Babangida administration.

In a petition dated 7 April 2010, and addressed to the new Attorney-General and Minister of Justice, Mohammed Bello Adoke, civil society groups threatened to go to court to compel the minister to prosecute Babangida. Contrary to Afegbua's claim that the missing money was spent on infrastructure in the Federal Capital Territory, Falana said there is no single reference in the report to back the claim that funds were spent to develop the Federal Capital Territory. He affirmed that the funds for Abuja were contained in the Federation Account.

One reason many Nigerians do not want Babangida to return to power is his corrupt nature; and his case will not be helped by the report published by Saharareporters on the Haliburton bribe scandal involving 80 eminent Nigerians. The list was obtained from five notebooks found on 2 September 2004 in the archives of the London office of Kellogg Brown & Root, KBR, by investigating Haliburton attorneys. The bribes were handed out in exchange for contracts at the Nigeria Liquefied Natural Gas project. The document, which was addressed to the Chairman of the Economic and Financial Crimes Commission, EFCC, lists former Nigerian heads of state, Ibrahim Babangida, Abdulsalami Abubakar, Sani Abacha, Ernest

Shonekan, as being on the list. Some of the other prominent Nigerians on the list are Maryam Babangida, Maryam Abacha, Dr. Rilwan Lukman, Alhaji Babagana Kingibe, Alhaji Aminu Saleh, Alhaji MD Yusufu, General Joshua Dogonyaro and Chief Don Etiebet among others.

Why many Nigerians are not disposed to a Babangida presidency this time is because of his laissez-faire attitude to corruption, something acknowledged at home and abroad. The book, The Sink, written by Jeffrey Robinson, an American, says: "Of the $120 billion siphoned out of the Nigeria into offshore accounts by dishonest politicians, $20 billion is allegedly traceable to IBB directly as president form 1985 to 1993". The World Bank and other sources put his loot at over $35 billion. In Karl Maiers' This House Has Fallen, former Inspector-General of Police, MD Yusufu noted that "Babangida went all out to corrupt society... This corruption remains and it is very corrosive to society."

The Gulf War oil windfall is Babangida's most celebrated loot. The Okigbo panel set up by Abacha discovered that only $206 million was left in the account and that "disbursements were clandestinely undertaken while the country was openly reeling with crushing external debt overhead... These represent, no matter the initial justification for creating the accounts, a gross abuse of public trust."

When in 2001, former president Olusegun Obasanjo tried to look into the $12.4 billion Gulf War oil windfall, it was said that the documents pertaining to the fraud had disappeared from the CBN records. However, in 2005 when the House of Representatives made moves to impeach Obasanjo, the documents which government sources claimed were missing, suddenly emerged. TheNEWS gathered that the documents were released at the time because Obasanjo's minders felt Babangida was one of those behind the plot.

Babangida's corrupt nature is legendary. The Wolfsberg Principles, an initiative of 11 banks and institutions across the world to fight serious international crimes, allegedly traced $3 billion of Nigeria's stolen money to Babangida's accounts abroad and $4.3b to Abacha's.

Although Babangida used mostly fictitious names for his numerous accounts abroad, EFCC could zero in on some of the accounts by following up on the dust raised early in 2003 over the financing of a leading Nigerian telecommunications project in which Babangida is alleged to own 75 per cent shares. Mohammed Babangida fronts for his father on the board of the company. Those claiming to have borrowed from foreign banks in the heat of the EFCC's revelations at the time have not identified the collateral used. Documents on the loan supposed to have been granted on 9 February 2001, were dated 28 August 2006. The original 'loan' letter has not been presented.

Luscious contracts for the construction of Abuja were awarded to front companies of his and his cronies, including Julius Berger and Arab Contractors. Between them, they virtually single-handedly handled the construction of the new Federal Capital. The security danger of foreign companies solely constructing a country's capital and having access to its structural secrets, including possible Presidential underground escape routes and military arsenal vaults, in the view of military experts, shows poor thinking.

It has often been stressed by his supporters that IBB is a patriot and acceptable to all the geo-political zones of the country. But this is largely exaggerated. Not many have forgotten how he brought Nigeria into the Organisation of Islamic Conference, OIC, without bringing the matter before the Armed Forces Ruling Council. The fact that he politicised the army, reserving most key appointments for the north, is one reason to believe he is both a religious and ethnic bigot. Though many have argued that he annulled the presidential election because he did not want to surrender power, the revelation of his son, Mohammed, that top northern army officers told him he must not handover to a southerner because "political power was all the north has" easily combusts this notion.

Besides, that he kept postponing his handing over date, despite committing billions of naira into the most expensive transition in history will also quash his "credentials" as a patriot. He simply continued to take Nigerians on a ride to nowhere, spending N40 billion on his endless transition programme.

A good number of Nigerians believe that the foundation for the depreciation of the Nigerian economy was laid during the Babangida years. He adopted the Structural Adjustment Programme, SAP, after throwing the matter to debate and it was resoundingly defeated by Nigerians, and proceeded to devalue the naira and pauperise the people. When he took power in 1985, it was N2 to a dollar, but by the time he left, it was about N60. That he accepted all the conditionalities of the International Monetary Fund and World Bank without giving a hoot about the implication still rankles. There is, in the estimation of analysts, no single facet of Nigeria's national life and moral fabric that IBB did not destroy. He is credited with the elimination of the middle class in Nigeria. He also targeted radicals. Those he could not compromise were either killed or hounded into exile. The killing of Dele Giwa, a frontline journalist, remains the classic of the genre. Though Babangida has continued to deny involvement in the death of Giwa, who was murdered via a parcel bomb in October 1986, the Oputa Panel set up to investigate Giwa's death indicted the former president. In a bid to fool Nigerians, the IBB regime set up panels and opened a case. But the case was just kept getting tossed from one investigating team to the other. This, naturally, yielded no result.

In fact, the Oputa Panel indicted IBB and his two security chiefs, Brigadier General Halilu Akilu and Colonel A.K. Togun. The panel recommended that for the nation to achieve full reconciliation, Giwa's case should be reopened for further investigations in the public interest. The report was part of the activities to mark the third anniversary of the restoration of democratic rule in the country. The report stated that, "On General Ibrahim Babangida, we are of the view that there is evidence to suggest that he and the two security chiefs are accountable for the death of Dele Giwa by letter bomb. We recommend that this case be re-opened for further investigation in the public interest." The commission's findings left IBB jittery. He headed for the courts to prevent the government from implementing the commission's recommendations.

Can he win?

Like all soldiers, Babangida has perfected the art of exploiting opportunities. Sources close to him told The NEWS last week that he was swayed to join the 2011 presidential race after he saw the turnout of people from all the geo-political zones, traditional rulers, military and even those opposed to him for years at his wife's burial in Minna last December. This convinced him that he has tremendous goodwill.

Babangida, who was once described by Professor Wole Soyinka as an "enemy of humanity and the humanities", saw what happened at his wife's funeral as practical demonstration of the fact that there is no Nigerian that has following like him across religion, age and other divides. The outpouring of emotions for him was all he needed.

Analysts spoken to last week noted that the greatest mistake anyone could make is to underrate IBB. "Nigeria is still underdeveloped. People are not influenced by ideology or principle in voting. Most of the time, the man who wins is the one who has tremendous resources; he has a lot of people he could call up to raise big money for his campaign," said a Lagos-based lawyer last Thursday. He described Babangida as the most destabilising force in today's Nigeria and that all the recycled kleptomaniacs in government today owe their wealth, influence and power to the "evil genius".

A preponderance of opinion sampled last week hinted at an emergent new political power base in Nigeria, i.e the Governors Forum. They warned that if IBB can get a majority of the governors on his side, he will most likely win.

"The governors are the most potent political set-up in contemporary Nigeria. I see him being supported by many of these unscrupulous governors. Some of them were even his boys. You can see that the likes of Uduaghan, Oyinlola, and Nyako are already with him. So, it all depends on where majority of these governors go," said Saleh Mohammed, a Sokoto-based public affairs analyst. He recalled that in 2003, IBB threw a wedding party for his first daughter. The event attracted 28 governors.

Another thing he has going for him is support of the traditional institution. While traditional rulers in the north dread Buhari, his rival, they are comfortable with Babangida. TheNEWS was told that the IBB strategists are confident that the traditional rulers, who are still very relevant at influencing public opinion and mobilising the masses, are going to support him when push comes to shove. A source reminded TheNEWS of how Sule Lamido lost the Jigawa governorship election in 1999 for the "crime" of threatening to deal with the "oppressive" traditional institution. He was the candidate to beat until he made that faux pas.

Analysts say it would take a very strong effort to stop IBB this time, as it is even suspected that Obasanjo, his kill-joy in 2006, is not against him this time. Buhari is thought to be a very formidable opponent in northern Nigeria, but lacks the financial wherewithal to win a national election. "Anything can happen. But it will be tough stopping IBB and I don't see him and his long-term friend Aliyu Gusau, the current National Security Adviser, going head-to-head," said an analyst.

Apart from the suspected pact with Obasanjo, who resisted every temptation to probe the Babangida years, there is the suspicion that he enjoys the support of the United States of America government. In its 4 March 2010 edition, The NATION, in an editorial asked President Barack Obama to stop flirting with Babangida. This followed the visit of Johnnie Carson, the US Assistant Secretary of State, and Robin Sanders, the US Ambassador to Nigeria, to Minna to confer with Babangida. The newspaper informed Obama that Babangida remains "one of the architects of Nigeria's present misfortune" and wondered what could have brought "a democrat and a dictator together". It was not long after the visit that IBB declared his interest in the 2011 presidential race. Could the Americans have goaded IBB to run? Can a Babangida presidency be strategic to American interests in Nigeria?

Abdulkarim Daiyabu, President of the Kano-based Movement of Justice in Nigeria, MOJIN, said Nigerians should be ready to fight to ensure IBB does not return to Aso Rock. "We have to mobilise and free ourselves from the likes of IBB who have stolen our country blind and want to keep us in perpetual servitude. This battle can only be won on the streets. I don't trust all our political parties because they are not different from the PDP. If we don't give this battle our best shot, a certified rogue like Babangida, who put us in the mess we are in right now, will emerge the winner," he warned.

There is every reason to believe that Nigerians are ready for the fight to keep the evil gap-toothed General out of power. His declaration of interest in the presidency has thrown up various groups that have employed the Internet to thwart the retired General's ambition. One of the groups, led by Modupe Debbie Ariyo, a U.K-based non-profit organisation leader, is strategising on how to halt IBB's return.

On Facebook alone, the group amassed over 2,500 active members in less than three days. The site has over 35 links to website and newspapers crusading against his return. The group claims that IBB's tenure as a military president witnessed the beginning of the collapse of Nigeria's economic and social fabric, marked by massive brain drain, breakdown of the educational system, unprecedented level of corruption and the annulment of the 12 June presidential election. Another group, National Democratic Forum, NDF, led by Jonathan Vatsa, the late General Mamman Vatsa's brother, is actively involved in the campaign to stop IBB. Already, the group is gearing towards a "Say No To IBB" campaign to begin in Benue State.

Still, websites like against babangida.com are already publishing reports of IBB's malfeasance in office. Many more groups are expected to join the fray as time goes on. Babangida surely thinks Nigerians are suffering from collective amnesia, and that all his sins, even if not forgiven are forgotten. The coming days will prove if that is truly the case.

APPENDIX III

Proving Babangida's Billions

Tunde Odediran

Ibrahim Babangida has thrown a challenge at Nigerians to prove that the billions of dollars he has personally acquired were not made through sheer hard work. He has boldly responded to charges of theft of public funds by demanding that those who make claims against him should prove the allegations or shut up.

Let's begin by making some quick deductions from Babangida's challenge. First, Babangida's has not said he does not have a lot of money. Secondly, and be careful in digesting this point, Babangida is not asserting he has not stolen public funds. And thirdly, the Evil Genius is not claiming his wealth has been acquired through legitimate means. The question he raised is not about honesty or integrity. All Babangida is saying is that whoever has the evidence should make it public; otherwise it is a closed case.

It is not at all surprising that the former dictator has chosen to use the conman's approach to wriggling his way out of the grave he dug for himself years ago. Regardless, the bold-face challenge is a change of tactics by the general, who has never before been in the habit of talking about his wealth. Babangida realizes that as a presidential candidate, if he ever becomes one, questions about his estate will come up. The statements are designed to quell those questions far in advance and set the tone for how he will brush off inquiries that sniff into the comfortable private life he has taken time to build and largely keep off pubic scrutiny.

In civilized societies, no person who seeks leadership position would so carelessly disrespect his potential employers by putting up not so much of a defense for an issue that is relevant and of active public interest.

Babangida's cold what-can-you-do response is just another slap in the soft face of Nigerians.

The case against Babangida and the thousands of military rulers who have stolen billions of Nigeria's dollars over the years is simple. It requires only basic accounting - calculate all of Babangida's lifetime income (salaries and interests on legitimate investments outlined in tax returns) and deduct all from his current assets. If he has accumulated more than he legitimately made, he has to prove the discrepancy.

Using this method, it will be so easy even for Babangida to make a case. The rest of the process will be for Babangida to prove the source of his remaining wealth. Nigerians will need to be told if won a huge lottery or money at a casino that enabled him to do the things he has done with money. The people are curious to know if he inherited much of his wealth from his dad or an uncle. The voters deserve to know how he has been able to support his ostentatious lifestyle.

The onus of proof, ultimately, for the legitimacy of Babangida's material acquisitions is not on Nigerians. It is on him. He has to prove where he got the money to build the multi-billion naira mansion on the exclusive hill top of Minna. He has to prove that his private aircrafts were cheaper than his total salaries with the Nigerian Army. He has to prove that all the properties and business under his name and that of his children were bought from his pension. He must prove that his estate abroad, running into billions of dollars, was bought with his naira-denominated income for the less than 30 years in public service.

After Babangida has proved how he acquired his wealth, Nigerians can then begin to ask him how the Gulf Oil windfall, which is now causing him serious headache, was spent. He has to explain how the debt buy-back deals during his regime were conducted. He has to explain which companies that got contracts during his administration are indirectly linked back to him. It will also be neccessary to adopt the same method to probe the wealth of Babangida's friends and family.

We throw Babangida's challenge back at him. He is the one who has a lot to explain.

APPENDIX IV

$12b Gulf War Oil Windfall – The Law Requires Babangida To Justify Or Forfeit His Unexplained Wealth

Hon. Justice Emmanuel Ayoola
Chairman, Independent Corrupt Practices Commission
Abuja

Sir,

<u>Petition to the ICPC: $12 Billion Gulf War Oil Windfall – The Law Requires Babangida to Justify or Forfeit His Unexplained Wealth</u>

1. You will no doubt be aware that the former military ruler, General Ibrahim Babangida, has announced his intention to contest next year's presidential election and has challenged his critics to prove their allegations that he enriched himself corruptly while in office, especially in relation to the $12.4 billion oil windfall earned by the country during the first Gulf War in 1991.

2. Fortunately, as a former public servant that boasts unexplained wealth, Babangida is plainly required by law to justify his wealth or forfeit it to the state. Therefore, the purpose of this petition is to instigate this procedure contained in section 44 of The Corrupt Practices and other Related Offences Act 2000 (the ICPC Act), which is designed to combat corruption and promote good governance.

3. You will recall that on 15th January 1994, the government of the late General Sani Abacha set up a panel of eminent Nigerians chaired by the late renowned economist, Dr. Pius Okigbo, (the

Panel on the Reorganisation and Reform of Central Bank of Nigeria) to probe how the $12.4 billion oil windfall was spent by Babangida's government. The panel's report was submitted to the government on 27th September, 1994.

4. It is on record, based on a summary of this report published by the government, that Babangida's regime conspired with top officials of the Central Bank of Nigeria (CBN) to squander this national fortune on unproductive or dubious projects, with $12.2 billion out of the $12.4 billion spent through "Dedicated Accounts" that were not available to auditors.

5. Although successive governments have refused to publish the full report, copies are widely available in the public domain and as the Chairman of the ICPC you should be able to obtain the full report the government.

6. However, the ICPC Act empowers you to request Babangida to either explain the legitimate sources of his enormous wealth or forfeit same to the state. The uncontroversial information disclosed by the government in relation to the Okigbo Panel's report is relevant but not strictly necessary evidence for this purpose.

7. Your Commission's website contains this very instructive information: "The ICPC Act 2000 brought a fresh and decisive perspective to the fight against corruption in the form of a holistic approach encompassing enforcement, prevention and educational measures. It captures in a single document, a host of corrupt (sic) offences in their old and sophisticated guises. It sets up the Independent Corrupt Practices and Other Related Offences Commission with wide-ranging powers."

8. One of these wide-ranging powers is your power under section 44 of the ICPC Act (which criminalises unexplained or illicit wealth) to subject any past or present government official to criminal penalties and forfeiture if in the course of an investigation you have reasonable grounds to believe that they committed a corruption offence.

9. It is clear from available information in relation the Okigbo panel's report that there are reasonable grounds to believe that serious corruption offences were committed under Babangida's watch with regards to the $12.4b Gulf War oil windfall. It is equally incontrovertible that Babangida is a man of great but unexplained wealth. His palatial Hilltop Mansion in Minna, the cost of which arguably exceeds the entire legitimate emoluments of his military and public service careers, stands as an obscene and poignant testament to this fact.

10. Therefore, as Babangida steps up his campaign to take charge of their affairs for a second time, the Nigerian public you serve as ICPC Chairman expect you, by virtue of section 44(1)(a) of the ICPC Act, to require him to provide a statement in writing on oath or affirmation in order to:

i. Identify every property, whether movable or immovable, whether within or outside Nigeria, belonging to him or in which he has any interest and specifying the date on which each of the properties so identified was acquired and the manner in which it was acquired;

ii. Identify every property transferred out of Nigeria by him during such period as may be specified in the notice;

iii. Set out the estimated value and location of each of the properties identified and if any of such properties cannot be located, the reason for this;

iv. State in respect of each of the properties identified whether the property is held by Babangida or by any other person on his behalf or whether it has diminished in value since its acquisition by him and whether it has been commingled with other property which cannot be separated or divided without difficulty;

v. Set out all other information relating to his properties, business, travel or other activities as may be specified in the notice; and

vi. Set out all his sources of income, including earnings and gifts or other assets for such period.

11. Section 44(1)(b) of the Act also empowers you to issue a similar notice to any relative or associate of Babangida or any other person whom you have   reasonable grounds to believe is able to assist in this investigation.

12. Furthermore, section 44(1)(c) of the Act authorises you to require any officer of any bank or financial institution to provide you with copies of all accounts, documents and records relating to Babangida or any of his relatives and associates once the above notice has been issued.

13. Significantly, section 44(2) of the Act provides that should you have reasonable grounds to believe that Babangida owns, possesses or controls any interest in any property which is excessive, having regard to his past emoluments and all other relevant circumstances, to require him by a written direction to provide a statement on oath or affirmation explaining how he was able to own, possess or control such excess. Furthermore, if he fails to explain satisfactorily such excess, he shall be presumed to have used his office to corruptly enrich or gratify himself and charged with corruption accordingly.

14. For completeness, it should be noted that section 44 (2) of the ICPC Act does not contravene the presumption of innocence guaranteed under section 36(5) of the 1999 Constitution. This is because section 36 makes clear that "nothing in this section shall invalidate any law by reason only that the law imposes upon any such person the burden of proving particular facts."

15. As you will no doubt be aware, the criminalization of illicit enrichment or inexplicable wealth under section 44 of the ICPC Act is a valuable tool for prosecuting corrupt leaders. It is also consistent with Nigeria's obligations under Article 20 of the United Nations Convention Against Corruption to adopt legislative and other measures necessary to establish illicit enrichment – a significant increase in the assets of a public official that he or she

cannot reasonably explain in relation to his or her lawful income - as a criminal offence.

16. It is therefore a source of great frustration to Nigerians that, like your predecessor, you have so far failed to invoke this very crucial provision despite the relentless distortion of our social, economic, legal and political systems by past and present corrupt leaders that continue to oppress us with their illicit wealth.

17. Under the circumstances, you will agree that the immediate enforcement of this legislation, starting with Babangida, will not only resolve the issue of the $12.4 billion oil windfall and determine his fitness to be entrusted with the affairs of the nation at this critical time but will also start the restoration of the ICPC as the apex anti-corruption body in Nigeria as intended by law.

18. I understand that this petition will be brought to your attention within 48 hours of the above date. I shall, therefore, look forward to hearing from you in due course.

Yours faithfully

Osita Mba

APPENDIX V

The Orkar Coup of April 22, 1990

By
Nowa Omoigui, MD

Nowa@prodigy.net

Shortly after dawn broke on April 22, 1990, the following broadcast was heard over the Federal Radio Corporation of Nigeria (FRCN) in Lagos:

"Fellow Nigerian Citizens,

On behalf of the patriotic and well-meaning peoples of the Middle Belt and the southern parts of this country, I , Major Gideon Orkar, wish to happily inform you of the successful ousting of the dictatorial, corrupt, drug baronish, evil man, deceitful, homo-sexually-centered, prodigalistic, un-patriotic administration of General Ibrahim Badamasi Babangida. We have equally commenced their trials for unabated corruption, mismanagement of national economy, the murders of Dele Giwa, Major-General Mamman Vatsa, with other officers as there was no attempted coup but mere intentions that were yet to materialise and other human rights violations.

The National Guard already in its formative stage is disbanded with immediate effect. Decrees Number 2 and 46 are hereby abrogated. We wish to emphasise that this is not just another coup but a well conceived, planned and executed revolution for the marginalised, oppressed and enslaved peoples of the Middle Belt and the south with a view to freeing ourselves and children yet unborn from eternal slavery and colonisation by a clique of this country.

Our history is replete with numerous and uncontrollable instances of callous and insensitive dominatory repressive intrigues by those who think it is their birthright to dominate till eternity the political and economic privileges of this great country to the exclusion of the people of the Middle Belt and the south.

They have almost succeeded in subjugating the Middle Belt and making them voiceless and now extending same to the south.

It is our unflinching belief that this quest for domination, oppression and marginalisation is against the wish of God and therefore, must be resisted with the vehemence.

Anything that has a beginning must have an end. It will also suffice here to state that all Nigerians without skeleton in their cupboards need not to be afraid of this change. However, those with skeleton in their cupboards have all reasons to fear, because the time of reckoning has come.

For the avoidance of doubt, we wish to state the three primary reasons why we have decided to oust the satanic Babangida administration. The reasons are as follows:

    (a) To stop Babangida's desire to cunningly, install himself as Nigeria's life president at all costs and by so doing, retard the progress of this country for life. In order to be able to achieve this undesirable goals of his, he has evidently started destroying those groups and sections he perceived as being able to question his desires.

Examples of groups already neutralised, pitched against one another or completely destroyed are:

        i. The Sokoto caliphate by installing an unwanted Sultan to cause division within the hitherto strong Sokoto caliphate.

ii. The destruction of the peoples of Plateau State, especially the Lantang people, as a balancing force in the body politics of this country.

iii. The buying of the press by generous monetary favours and the usage of State Security Service, SSS, as a tool of terror.

iv. The intent to cow the students by the promulgation of the draconian decree Number 47.

v. The cowing of the university teaching and non-teaching staff by an intended massive purge, using the 150 million dollar loan as the necessitating factor.

vi. Deliberately withholding funds to the armed forces to make them ineffective and also crowning his diabolical scheme through the intended retrenchment of more than half of the members of the armed forces.

Other pointers that give credence to his desire to become a life president against the wishes of the people are:

(1) His appointment of himself as a minister of defence, his putting under his direct control the SSS, his deliberate manipulation of the transition programme, his introduction of inconceivable, unrealistic and impossible political options, his recent fraternisation with other African leaders that have installed themselves as life presidents and his dogged determination to create a secret force called the national guard, independent of the armed forces and the police which will be answerable to himself alone, both operationally and administratively.

It is our strong view that this kind of dictatorial desire of Babangida is unacceptable to Nigerians of the 1990's, and, therefore, must be resisted by all.

(b)   Another major reason for the change is the need to stop intrigues, domination and internal colonisation of the Nigerian state by the so-called chosen few. This, in our view, has been and is still responsible for 90 percent of the problems of Nigerians. This indeed has been the major clog in our wheel of progress.

This clique has an unabated penchant for domination and unrivalled fostering of mediocrity and outright detest for accountability, all put together have been our undoing as a nation.

This will ever remain our threat if not checked immediately. It is strongly believed that without the intrigues perpetrated by this clique and misrule, Nigeria will have in all ways achieved developmental virtues comparable to those in Korea, Taiwan, Brazil, India, and even Japan.

Evidence, therefore, this cancerous dominance has as a factor constituted by a major and unpardonable clog in the wheel of progress of the Nigerian state. (Sic) It is suffice to mention a few distasteful intrigues engineered by this group of Nigerians in recent past. These are:

1. The shabby and dishonourable treatment meted on the longest serving Nigerian general in the person of General Domkat Bali, who in actual fact had given credibility to the Babangida administration.

2. The wholesale hijacking of Babangida's administration by the all powerful clique.

3. The disgraceful and inexplicable removal of Commodore Ebitu Ukiwe, Professor Tam David-West, Mr. Aret Adams and so on from office.

4. The now-pervasive and on-going retrenchment of Middle Belt and southerners from public offices and their instant replacement by the favoured class and their stooges.

5. The deliberate disruption of the educational culture and retarding its place to suit the favoured class to the detriment of other educational minded parts of this country.

6. The deliberate impoverishment of the peoples from the Middle Belt and the south, making them working ghosts and feeding on the formulae of 0-1-1- or 0-0-0 while the aristocratic class and their stooges are living in absolute affluence on a daily basis without working for it.

7. Other countless examples of the exploitative, oppressive, dirty games of intrigues of its class, where people and stooges that can best be described by the fact that even though they contribute very little economically to the well being of Nigeria, they have over the years served and presided over the supposedly national wealth derived in the main from the Middle Belt and the southern part of this country, while the people from these parts of the country have been completely deprived from benefiting from the resources given to them by God.

(c) The third reason for the change is the need to lay a strong egalitarian foundation for the real democratic take off of the Nigerian state or states as the circumstances may dictate.

In the light of all the above and in recognition of the negativeness of the aforementioned aristocratic factor, the overall progress of the Nigerian state a temporary decision to excise the following states namely, Sokoto, Borno, Katsina, Kano and Bauchi states from the Federal Republic of Nigeria comes into effect immediately until the following conditions are met.

The conditions to be met to necessitate the re-absorption of the aforementioned states are as following:

i. To install the rightful heir to the Sultanate, Alhaji Maccido, who is the people's choice.

ii. To send a delegation led by the real and recognised Sultan Alhaji Maccido to the federal government to vouch that the feudalistic and aristocratic quest for domination and operation will be a thing of the past and will never be practised in any part of the Nigeria state.

By the same token, all citizens of the five states already mentioned are temporarily suspended from all public and private offices in Middle Belt and southern parts of this country until the mentioned conditions above are met.

They are also required to move back to their various states within one week from today. They will, however, be allowed to return and joint the Federal Republic of Nigeria when the stipulated conditions are met.

In the same vein, all citizens of the Middle Belt and the south are required to come back to their various states pending when the so-called all-in-all Nigerians meet the conditions that will ensure a united Nigeria. A word is enough for the wise.

This exercise will not be complete without purging corrupt public officials and recovering their ill-gotten wealth, since the days of the oil boom till date. Even in these hard times, when Nigerians are dying from hunger, trekking many miles to work for lack of transportation, a few other Nigerians with complete impunity are living in unbelievable affluence both inside and outside the country.

We are extremely determined to recover all ill-gotten wealth back to the public treasury for the use of the masses of our people. You are all advised to remain calm as there is no cause for alarm. We are fully in control of the situation as directed by God. All airports, seaports and borders are closed forthwith.

The former Armed Forces Ruling Council is now disbanded and replaced with National Ruling Council to be chaired by the head of state with other members being a civilian vice-head of state, service chiefs, inspector general of police, and one representative each from NLC, NUJ, NBA, and NANS. A curfew is hereby imposed from 8 p.m. to 6 a.m. until further notice. All members of the armed forces and the police forces are hereby confined to their respective barracks. All unlawful and criminal acts by those attempting to cause chaos will be ruthlessly crushed. Be warned as we are prepared at all costs to defend the new order. All radio stations are hereby advised to hook on permanently to the national network programme until further notice.

Long live all true patriots of this great country of ours. May God and Allah through his bountiful mercies bless us all."

APPENDIX VI

Marwa Deliver the Bomb To Dele Giwa?

In the word of Professor Taiyemiwo Ogunade, published by one of the credible on line media, Saharareporters, the killers of Dele Giwa is here with us, desiring to lead us again. Saharareporters: Do you know who delivered the bomb that killed Dele Giwa?

Ogunade: I believe that Buba Marwa did it. Some Mamman Vatsa boys told the full story in New York during a visit to my college to lobby our college to accept to train Nigerian military officers. Ambassador Olusola was on that entourage. [My informant] told me Dele Giwa was killed because he was in possession of a tape containing Vatsa's testimony before the military tribunal. For four hours, Vatsa requested to tell the full story about how the Babangida regime was operating and his knowledge of the workings of IBB's mind. He pointed out that after Halilu Akilu and Col. A.K Togun of the military intelligence prepared the parcel it was handed over to Buba Marwa to deliver to Dele Giwa. Marwa is a well-known "IBB boy". But I was the one who gave Dele Giwa the tape.

Saharareporters: How did you get the tape?

Ogunade: Vatsa had a copy made by his friends in the tribunal and smuggled out to me and I "loaned" it to Dele Giwa who got on the case immediately. I still don't know how Dele Giwa found out that I had the tape till this day.

Saharareporters: Do you still have a copy?
Ogunade: Yes, but you know I left Nigeria hurriedly after the death of Dele Giwa. I left [the tape] with my aged mother, who did not know the value then. I won't say more, let the military release that tape to the Nigerian public.

Saharareporters: Did Dele Giwa return the tape to you?

Ogunade: Yes, he returned it after 24 hours. Don't forget that I loaned it to him; I think he went and played it to Babangida's people and they eliminated him after they heard the tape.

Saharareporters: What about Gloria Okon? It's been said that Dele Giwa's discovery of her was the reason he was killed?

Ogunade: Gloria Okon is actually Chinyere, that's her real name. She married Charles "Jeff" Chandler, the fellow who killed Nzeogwu and was killed a day later. Chinyere, Maryam and Princess Atta were young friends who hung out together. They all married into the military, because the military was a proud and respectable profession then. Charles Chandler, who was Tiv, married Chinyere who I think is from Imo State. IBB married Maryam from Asaba and Mamman Vatsa married the princess. So Chinyere became a widow and resorted to trading between UK and Nigeria. And then she was caught with drugs; Mamman Vatsa was the person who put Chinyere on the next available flight from Kano to London – and then claimed that she was dead by parading a dead woman picked out of the mortuary. Dele Giwa later found out that she was in London having delivered a baby by another man. He sent a French photographer to the place and they saw Maryam Babangida at the event. Kayode Soyinka brought back the photographs. Dele was sitting across the table from Kayode examining the photos taken of "Gloria Okon" (Chinyere, Richard Chandler's wife) at the naming ceremony in London. Maryam Babangida was there. And then a letter parcel was delivered to him and he said excitedly that it must be from "Mr. President" referring to the discussions he had with IBB days earlier. The bomb exploded and severed his lower abdomen; he died a few hours later.

Saharareporters: Did you ever meet Marwa again? And did you ask him about his involvement?

Ogunade: Yes, Marwa was very active in the Nigerian embassy in New York. For a long time he was the "military attaché" to the Nigerian mission in New York while I was a professor of Black Studies at the City University of New York. He came to my college to sign a $30 million contract with the college so that members of the Nigerian military could attend a "Peace and Conflict Resolution program" and then be awarded a masters degree upon completion of the program. I fought bitterly against it, but the chair of the department, John Muyibi Amoda, badly wanted the money. I kept fighting and one day the college authorities acceded to my request.

When I got home the college had dismissed me, but also I got a fax message saying the $30 million had been returned to Marwa. But between Marwa and Abacha they never returned that money to the Nigerian treasury. They shared it. I heard between him and Abacha, over $250 million was laundered through an account used by the New York mission of the Nigerian embassy. Marwa later set up an airline with his share of the loot. When he showed up to run for president I was the one who petitioned the Economic and Financial Crimes Commission (EFCC) to investigate him. He confessed to money laundering in handwritten statements to the EFCC, but today he is the ambassador of Nigeria to South Africa. The police officer that investigated him, Ibrahim Magu, is permanently suspended from the police force after he was humiliated by the EFCC. It is a shameful country.

APPENDIX VII

Day of the Owner Catches Up With IBB

Next

After years of prevarication by several governments, the chicken might be coming home to roost for Ibrahim Babangida. NEXT gathered in Abuja, the seat of power, last night, that the Federal Government has raised a committee to probe the eight-year military government of Mr. Babangida. The former military president is alleged to have mismanaged over $12.4 billion that accrued from crude oil sales during the Gulf War.

The Attorney-General of the Federation and Minister of Justice, Mohammed Bello Adoke (SAN), told our correspondent in a telephone conversation that the committee is chaired by the Solicitor-General of the Federation and Permanent Secretary in the Federal Ministry of Justice, Abdulahi Yola.
Although the committee has been charged to work expeditiously to meet the huge expectations of the citizens, it was learnt that it has no deadline, however.

Mr. Adoke's revelation came on the trail of renewed actions being made to push for the enforcement of zoning as a political means of picking the presidential candidate of the Peoples' Democratic Party (PDP) from the north in 2011 by a 48-man team inaugurated on Sunday at a meeting held by the Northern Elders' Forum. One of the people who was nominated into the group of eminent personalities and who could be the key beneficiary of a successful rapprochement is Mr. Babangida, a retired General seeking to reclaim power in 2011, after "stepping aside" on August 27, 1993.

Mr. Adoke says: "The committee on Okigbo report has been constituted. The committee's work will begin properly as soon as the Solicitor-General of the Federation, who is the chairman of the committee, and who, right now, is away on an official assignment outside the country, returns. "The committee will begin the process of its work by first authenticating the copy of the report we received. Once that is done, it will go ahead to review all the allegations and recommendations in the report, with a view to advising the Federal Government on the next line of action."

The Justice Minister declined to authorise his Media Assistant or the Ministry's Chief Press Secretary to release the names of the other members of the committee. "The work of the committee is a very sensitive one. So, it is not right for me at this stage to reveal or authorise any of my aides to disclose the names of the other members for the simple reason that they could be exposed to high level of risks, influence peddling, following a public knowledge, and the possibility of tampering with the document and result," Mr. Adoke added. With the inauguration of the committee, the Justice Minister has fulfilled his promise to set up a committee that will determine the authenticity of the Pius Okigbo Panel report, and review the allegations and recommendations, with a view to ascertaining whether the allegations can sustain a criminal charge against Mr. Babangida.

Mr. Adoke had on May 12 acknowledged the receipt of the certified true copy of the report a group of civil society organisations (CSOs) sent to him.

A coalition of CSOs on May 5, 2010, fulfilled its promise to dust and produce the certified true copy (CTC) of Okigbo Panel Report accusing Mr. Babangida of embezzling $12.4 billion, after Mr. Adoke requested for the original copy that was alleged by the government of former president Olusegun Obasanjo to be missing. The group of CSOs comprises: the Socio-Economic Rights and Accountability Project, Women Advocates and Documentation Centre, Access to Justice, Committee for Defence of Human Rights, Civil Society Legislative Advocacy Centre, Partnership for Justice, Human and Environmental Development Agenda, Nigeria Liberty Forum, Nigeria Voters Assembly, and Centre for the Rule of Law.

Meanwhile, in pursuance of his dream, Mr. Babangida, who has vowed to contest the next presidential election whether he is picked by the PDP or not, will on Thursday unveil his vision for a national rebirth at a one-day summit being organised by the National Solidarity Association, in Kaduna.

APPENDIX VIII

IBB is Mr. Inconsistency - Abiola's Daughter

The Punch
Daughter of M.K.O. Abiola, Mrs. Hafsat Abiola-Costello, has described Nigeria's former military dictator, General Ibrahim Babangida, as a case study of policy and administrative inconsistencies. Hafsat recalled that IBB's eight years of administration between 1985 and 1993 was marred by betrayal of public interest.

"So, I don't think that the issue is not whether or not he can run next year. As a citizen of Nigeria, all Nigerians obviously have the legal rights to run. What we should be looking at is, what IBB's problem was at the time he was governing Nigeria for eight years, such that when he would be doing what seemed good for the country at the last minute he would change course." She opined that IBB's behaviour could suggest a fundamental psychological problem, adding "I am sorry to be so blunt, but when I analysed the issue carefully, I don't see any other possible conclusion."

Abiola-Costello whose mother, Alhaja Kudirat Abiola, was assassinated on June 4, 1996, wondered what could have made IBB to drag Nigerians through seemingly laudable programmes only for him to abandon the course. "Is it that he does not respect the Nigerian country and the Nigerian people? Or is it that there is a mental default that makes it difficult for him to follow through on his action?" she queried.

She added, "Whatever conclusion this analysis is, should then determine for him how he should continue in 2011. **If the conclusion is that there is a mental defect, clearly, he should go for psychiatric help and if the conclusion is that he does not take the country seriously, then he should not even be considering running. Either way, I don't see how he should consider running."**

APPENDIX IX

Why I Am Hunted by IBB, by Bashorun

Punch

Major Debo Basorun was the military press secretary to Ibrahim Babangida (retd.). In this interview with NIYI ODEBODE of The Punch, he opens up on his ordeals in the hands of the former dictator and the death of Dele Giwa.

Under what circumstances did you leave the army?

There was a threat to my life and that is what this brouhaha is all about. I was privy to some of the terrible things Babangida and Akilu did when we were in the army. There was this determination on their path to silence me. I was surprised when I saw my name in the newspapers two weeks ago. They said I was wanted. That is far from the truth. I resigned from the army.

You said you were privy to some information. What information?

My problem is 2011. Babangida wants to become president again. I am not saying I am the only person, but I am one of those who know that he is connected to the death of Dele Giwa. That is why they have been trying to kill me.

When did you leave the army?

I resigned on December 28, 1988. I joined the army as a private on September 1, 1967 and commanded two battalions during the civil war. I was an infantry soldier. My first station was the 17, Infantry Battalion Iwo Road, Ibadan. From there, I volunteered to go to the war front. I served with 72 Infantry Battalion at Asaba. I was in the Nigerian troops that crossed to Onitsha on the third attempt. After a few months in Onitsha, I was injured and brought back to Ibadan . From Ibadan , I was brought back to Lagos . In Lagos , I was attached to Rehabilitation Centre at Oshodi. From there, I was taken to the Third Marine Commando Division. In the Third Marine Commando Division, I served in the 12 and 14 battalions. In 1979, I was the spokesperson for the United Nations in the Middle East. My last unit was at Dodan Barracks. I was the military press secretary to Gen. Ibrahim Babangida.

What has happened since your return from exile?

There had been two chiefs of army staff since I came back from exile before the present one. I went into exile in 1989 and the first time I came back to the country was 2006. I stayed briefly in the country and went back. When I came back fully in 2007, I met with IBB at a social function. I have been in trouble since, because I did not exchange pleasantries with him at the social function. He has been sending people to harass me. I have been ignoring him up to a point. I had to cry out in the media and grant an interview to a newspaper. Since then, they have been saying that they will deal with me for trying to spill the beans. Is it because of 2011? The man is so desperate now. His think tank has warned him that if I am still circulating about, there is every chance that I will abort his ambition. Come to think of it. What is important about Debo Bashorun? Is the army trying to tell me that since 20 years that I have left the army, there has been nobody who has gone on AWOL (absence without leave)? How many people have they advertised that they are looking for? When they started this nonsense, they said that I stole money before I left the army. If I stole money, let them hand over their documents to the police; the Economic and Financial Crimes Commission or the Independent Corrupt Practices and Other Related Offences Commission. Let me be tried in a court of law. I am not going to surrender myself to any of them. I am telling you authoritatively that Babangida has given instructions that once they grab me, they should poison me. I am not going to allow that to happen to me. Remember what happened to Chief Moshood Abiola. I want the world to hear what is going on. He has an ambition to be the president. One of his lieutenants know that I am about to publish a book. If I did not desert the army during the turbulent days of civil war, how would I desert when I was enjoying?

You have not explained how you left the army.

I was sent to do a dirty job in America in respect of Dele Giwa's death. I was sent to cover up what they did. I refused to comply. When I came back they threw me into jail. Newspapers reported it that time. I protested. The press was on my side then. I was shouting on the roof top that "These people want to kill me." They decided to send me to a unit in Makurdi, which was a Siberia then. I refused to go. Incidentally, the General Staff Headquarters, which was my unit (and Babangida's unit too), issued an order that whoever wanted to leave the army should volunteer. It coincided with what was happening to me. So I volunteered and resigned. I quoted their order in the resignation letter I sent them. But out of those who resigned then, I was the only person whose resignation was rejected. I contacted some attorneys. Alao Aka-Basorun was my lawyer. Femi Falana was his two-in-c (second-in-command). I told them I wanted to leave the army because I was privy to what the two people (IBB and Akilu) had been doing. I said that I was tired of it and did not want to be part of it any longer. My lawyers reviewed the law and said that there was nothing preventing me from leaving the army. So I resigned, but they rejected my resignation. I am getting close to 70.

Why did the army say you are a deserter in spite of the fact that you resigned?

Of course, 2011 is the issue. Babangida has assembled a think tank of south-westerners who have warned him of my tell-all book that is about to be launched. They warned him that if I am allowed to launch the book, the expose contained there will totally destroy his chances of even gaining a foothold any where in the South-West.

What do you think of Babangida's presidential ambition?

That is a disaster waiting to happen. He is just coming for a vengeance. People that have criticised him will be in terrible trouble. What did he leave that he was coming to take? I know him very well. I was close to him. I was involved in his life. I was involved in his wife's personal life. If he comes back, the county will be sold.

What was in your mind during IBB's transition programme?

I never believed him. In fact, I told Chief Abiola, God is my witness that he should not rely on him.

APPENDIX X

Ghost of June 12 Must Haunt Babangida, says Oyedepo, Bishops

The Guardian

Presiding Bishop of the Winners' Chapel, Dr. David Oyedepo, has said the ghost of the annulled June 12, 1993, presidential election will continue to haunt self-styled military president, Gen. Ibrahim Babangida, for life. The cleric said Nigerians are wiser than Babangida and have not forgotten the pains he inflicted on them through the cancellation of the polls adjudged to have been won by the late business mogul, Chief Moshood Kashimawo Olawale (M.K.O.) Abiola.

Also, the Methodist Bishops in Nigeria rose yesterday from a three-day conference in Kaduna condemning Babangida's interest in the 2011 presidential election. In a statement signed by the Prelate of the Methodist Church in Nigeria, Dr. Sunday Ola Makinde and the Conference Secretary, Rev. Raphael Opoko, the church said Babangida's move to lead the country under a democratic setting was an insult on Nigerians. They said Babangida's annulment of the freest and fairest election Nigeria ever conducted led to the death and misery of millions of Nigerians. In a message to mark the church 29th anniversary last Sunday at Faith Tabernacle, Canaanland, Ota in Ogun State, Oyedepo said there is no amount of repackaging that can make any difference or change Nigerians' perception of Babangida as "an anti-democratic person." He said: "*Babangida is anti-democratic. There is no repackaging of this man than can change anything. You cannot repackage Babangida and Babangida cannot be repackaged. If you mention the name Babangida any day, Nigerians will remember the annulment of June 12 presidential election.*"

Turning to the congregation, Oyedepo said "*if there is anyone in this church that associates with Babangida, you must retrace your steps immediately. This is an order not a plea. If any member of this church in any part of the world is found associating with Babangida, he will be taken for deliverance because only insane people can follow him." Oyedepo continued: "If there is anyone that sees Babangida, please tell him that I (Oyedepo) say he is wasting his time. If the Peoples Democratic Party (PDP), the All Nigeria Peoples Party (ANPP) or any other party thinks that Babangida is the person they have to present to Nigerians, then such a party is heading for doom."*

Makinde, who addressed journalists after the 28th yearly conference of the Methodist bishops, said it was during the tenure of Babangida that corruption became a status symbol among Nigerian leaders. In a 12-point statement, the bishops sought autonomy for the Independent National Electoral Commission (INEC) so that the 2011 elections will be hitch-free. Makinde said: *"The news of the declaration of the former military dictator, Gen. Ibrahim Babangida that he will run for the presidency of the country at the forthcoming elections is an insult to the generality of Nigerians because President Ibrahim Babaginda annulled the freest and fairest elections held in Nigeria in 1993 which led to the death and misery of millions of Nigerians."Council noted that it was during his tenure that the level of corruption was raised to the level which has almost sunk the country,"* he said.

APPENDIX XI

IBB's money rips NIDO apart

Saharareporters.com
A plan by some executive members of the government sponsored Nigerian In Diaspora Organization (NIDO) to adopt former military dictator, Ibrahim Babangida, as the presidential candidate of the group at their annual conference in Minna, Babangida's hometown, is ripping the hardly representative group apart. Saharareporters is in possession of a series of correspondence between the UK-based "leader" of the group, the owner of BENTV in London, Alistair Soyode, and otherof its leaders who are raging over last-minute shift of the annual meeting of the group to Minna. Mr. Soyode is accused of working with the ex-husband of Iyabo Obasanjo, the daughter of Nigeria's former president, Akeem Folajimi Bello and one lady Known as Folashade Arowoselu. Alistair is a well-known hustler who transverses Nigerian state capitals paying solidarity visits to corrupt public officials.

Mr. Folajimi Bello has had a fair share of ethical troubles too. In 2005, as a result of his engaging in securities malfeasance, Bello was fined about $26,000 by the National Association Of Securities Dealers (NASD), which also suspended him for one year. NASD claimed unethical practices on the part of Bello, saying he "made unsuitable recommendations to public customers and engaged in outside business activities for compensation without providing prompt written notice to his member firm."

Bello's suspension began on May 16, 2005, and should have concluded at the close of business on May 15, 2006. However, he left that job to run a political party in Nigeria known as New Democrats under whose banner he ran as a candidate in 2007 elections.

In 2008, NIDO was embroiled in a major land scandal involving a so-called "Diaspora Village" carved out for the organization in Abuja. There is still a series of petitions by some members who claimed the leaders of the organization duped them over the land allocated to the organization by the Obasanjo regime.

In 2007, the president of NIDO-Europe, a prominent Nigerian dentist, Dr. Femi Olojugba, was jailed for 18 months in the United Kingdom for perpetrating medial fraud.

On the subject of holding the annual meeting in Minna, two leading members of the organization have now called for a major campaign against the move by Soyode and his group to sell "NIDO" to Babangida. The members are Benson Osawe and Nweke Collins. In several emails to other members, they have waged a strong battle against Mr. Soyode and his cohorts, insisting that the Diaspora Day event, which is aimed at marking Nigeria's 50th Independence anniversary, remain in Abuja.

Babangida's campaign to return to the presidency has attracted widespread condemnation by Nigerians. Based on the high level of rejection of his candidacy, IBB, as he is widely known, had by last week began to jettison the idea, but sources told Saharareporters that he sees an interview held by Soyode's BENTV outfit to whitewash IBB's horrendous record is seen as a ray of hope. His minions also calculate that if Nigerians in the "Diaspora" led by Mr. Soyode endorse him, he would use that as a basis for re-igniting his suffocating campaign.

APPENDIX XII

Many Shun image publishing Book Launch

PM News & The Nation
Former military ruler, Gen. Ibrahim Babangida, is fighting hard to make himself appealing by launching a book crafted to change public opinion about how he misruled Nigeria. His stooge is the Director of the Centre for Democratic Development, Research and Training, Dr. Abubakar Mohammed, who hepled write the book titled: "Impressions And Facts About IBB's Govt: 1985-1993." The book captures the events in the Babangida government, with a clear intention to make the outcome of the regime better than it was. The event was largely avoided by notable invitees. According to the author, some of the impressions of the IBB regime are mere fantasies and the purpose of the book, therefore is not just to go beyond the myth of 'Maradona'; evil genius and institutionalization corruption which IBB is credited with, but to unambiguously state the facts as they are.

Saddique maintained that the book is not a biography or autobiography but a study and research on the government he headed, adding that the book is purely without any input from IBB and that he has presented issues as they are, explicitly stating both the rights and wrongs of the regime. While defending the allusion that the idea behind the book was to kick start the process of cleansing the perceived "dirty image" of the retired General, Saddique stated that the book is the first in the series that will also in the future carry out studies on the regimes of other leaders before and after the IBB's. This notwithstanding, there are however, arguments as to why the author started the supposed series with the regime of IBB as against those before him. The conclusion, to observers is that the book was deliberately released to coincide with the presidential bid of the General.

Eminent personalities failed to turn up as expected at the book launch. Governors, ministers, traditional rulers, top business men and many others personalities across the country shunned the event expected to boost IBB's political campaign and public rating.

However, Chief Tony Eze the chief launcher, a big time businessman during the military era donated N10 million in support of the book entitled: "Impression and Facts: Nigeria under General Ibrahim Badamasi Babangida, 1985-1993." Notable personalities present other that IBB himself included former Inspector General of Police, Alhaji M. D. Yusuf and former Information Minister, Chief Alex Akinyele. The Emir of Zazzau, Alhaji Shehu Idris and his counterpart in Katsina sent representatives to the ceremony that was attended by scores of not-too-privileged Nigerians. The book launch was held at the International Conference Centre in the federal capital city.

APPENDIX XIII

<u>**Clerics Spreading Anti-IBB Messages**</u>

Punch

The Presiding Bishop of The Redeemed Evangelical Mission, Bishop Mike Okonkwo, has urged Nigerians not to support the presidential ambition of the former military dictator, Gen. Ibrahim Babangida. Okonkwo's call follows the path laid by Pastor Tunde Bakare of the Save Nigeria Group. He advised IBB to forget the ambition. According to him, IBB ruled the nation for about eight years and played some unsavoury roles, especially in the annulment of June 12, 1993 election won by the late Chief MKO Abiola.

In a media briefing in Lagos on Saturday, Okonkwo who is a former Vice-Chairman, Christian Association of Nigeria and former President, Pentecostal Fellowship of Nigeria, said the Christian community had started mobilising against IBB's presidential ambition. According to him, younger politicians should be encouraged and given chance to rule the nation, stating tghat it was the global trend.

"IBB should sit down. He has had his turn. He should sit down and advise the government and let the young people come up and do it. What else will he give us that others cannot give us? We are also aware of the role he played. People should not give him a chance. Anybody that endorses IBB is doing that because of what he can get and not that he really loves him. If he loves himself, he should honourably retire."

APPENDIX XIV

The Master Manipulator

Financial Times of London

A former military ruler of Nigeria with a reputation as a political kingpin and "master manipulator" plans to emerge from the shadows and seek the presidency at the next election. General Ibrahim Baban-gida appears to be capitalising on a leadership crisis in sub-Saharan Africa's biggest energy producer. The polls, due in the first half of next year, promise to be the most competitive since the army handed back power to civilians in 1999. "He will contest," Kassim Afegbua, spokesman for Gen Babangida, told the Financial Times yesterday. "The country is sharply divided. We need a man who is a rallying point."

The former general, popularly known by his initials "IBB", retains unrivalled connections in a country where power is secured through a vast patronage network. Gen Babangida seized power in a bloodless coup in 1985 and critics say that corruption became allpervasive during his eight-year rule. He relinquished control in 1993 amid a wave of unrest following his annulment of a general election. Now 68, Gen Babangida has been plotting his return ever since. Most recently, he declared his intention to run in the last elections in 2007 before withdrawing. For all his influence, some analysts said, the former general could struggle to win over a country where memories of military rule are still fresh.

He faces younger challengers and it is unclear whether he is acting in alliance with Olusegun Obasanjo, the ex-military leader and former civilian president who vies with Gen Babangida for the mantle of Nigeria's political titan. From his north-eastern home town of Minna, Gen Babangida remains central to the powerful security apparatus. One foreign official said: "If you want to be promoted general, you have to go to Minna first."

Gen Babangida is reputed to have amassed significant wealth. Earlier this month activist groups demanded court action against him over an alleged $12.2bn (€8.98bn, £7.9bn) hole in the country's oil windfall from the price rise triggered by the 1990-91 Gulf war. The former leader's spokesman denied the allegations. Gen Babangida will seek the nomination of the ruling People's Democratic party at primary elections expected by November. But half a dozen former security chiefs, state governors and senior politicians are also jockeying for the PDP ticket. The dark horse is Goodluck Jonathan, the acting president. Previously little known, he has consolidated his authority since Mr Yar'Adua's disappearance, muscling out members of the stricken leader's inner circle. Yet Gen Babangida will have a hand in the outcome, regardless of whether he triumphs. As one of his former ministers put it: "He is the master manipulator."

APPENDIX XV

Nigeria in Diaspora kick against Babangida

In the United States, the Nigeria People's Parliament in Diaspora unanimously passed a resolution early this year, asking the Federal Government to prosecute Babangida and ban him from holding public office for annulling the June 12 election. The parliament, which first convened in March, passed the resolutions during its second plenary session held at the Bailey Theater Hall of the LaGuardia Crowne Plaza in the Queens District of New York. The Nigeria Democratic Liberty Forum convened the parliament. The resolutions followed several motions moved by some of the over 80 parliamentarians at the session.

Omoyele Sowore, publisher of Saharareporters.com said: "We must ensure that we find out from Babangida before he dies why he was so cowardly and those people who put a gun to his head to annul that election must be identified; they must be scrutinised, interrogated and appropriately punished." Sowore said Babangida should be banned from politics and public life. Besides, he should be arrested and tried for annulling the democratic aspiration of 150 million people, he said, adding that the Economic and Financial Crimes Commission (EFCC) should probe the corruption allegations against him. Another member of the parliament, Olusegun Dare, said: "We should make a motion here, declaring him as enemy of progress, enemy of democracy and enemy of Nigeria." The motions were put to vote and passed unanimously. Alex Kabba, the publisher of Africans Abroad-USA, a New York newspaper, moved a motion for the recognition of those who fought fearlessly for democracy during the 1993 election.

APPENDIX XVI

The Ibrahim Badamasi Babangida Saga

Written by Ndiameeh Babrik
Ordinarily, one would not bother to write on or about IBB in the Nigerian contemporary discourse since he is a failed military Head of State and a failed and a disgraced general. But at every turn of event, he has many paid sycophants and paid agents who will continue to dish out blatant lies to try to re-write and turn history on its heads. At this age and time where every and all informations are at everybody's finger tips, it is still surprising that Babangida and his agents can still lie in the village square.

Take IBB's BBC Hausa Service interview for example. He blatantly lied that he met the Naira selling for 4.5 to the US dollar. We do not expect a former military Head of State who even desires to rule Nigeria again to lie on petty issues like the Naira exchange rate in 1985. Babangida is said to be about 69 years now. If at this age he can lie on petty things like that, what morals will he teach his children and grandchildren? Let us assume again that in his dreams he becomes the Head of State of Nigeria, it is then clear to all Nigerians that his government will be built on lies and deceit. For the information of the readers of this article, as at 27th August 1985 when IBB staged his coup, the Naira was exchanging 0.765 Naira= one US dollar. But by the time he was chased out of Aso Rock Villa by bloody civilians on 26th August 1993, the Naira was exchanging for 21.9 Naira to one US dollars. Source: Central Bank of Nigeria at www.cenbank.org, Http://web.archive.org.That is one of the many lies of IBB.

As a sane human being one will start wondering on what ground Babangida wants the Nigerian government to immortalise Chief MKO Abiola. Unfortunately some of us are never opportuned to come close to the disgrace general to put some of these questions across to him. The way

Babangida opens his mouth tells everyone truly that he is a man without conscience.

But I don't blame IBB, the youth he has castigated for lack of quality education and leadership though through no fault of theirs is the same youth now busy campaigning for IBB to come and finish his unfinished job he started in 1985 and was abruptly terminated by force of civilians in 1993. To be fair to the Nigerian youth it is only some misguided few. But if IBB was still interested in power why did he quit it in 1993? There was no military coup against him, he did not conduct an election and honorably handed over to the winner like OBJ or Abdulsalami. Why did he leave power unceremoniously then? But on what basis is he advocating for Chief MKO Abiola to be immortalized now? Is it on the basis of the fact that he was the winner of the June 12 1993 election? What a self indictment by IBB. You see, the truth has a way of bringing itself to the fore.

Coming to those defending Babangida that he was rich before he became military Head of State. Going through Babangida's biography, you will discover that he was orphaned at 4 years and was brought up by his uncle. Joined the army at 21 years and he bought his first Vespa motor cycle as an Army Major in 1969/70. All his life he was a military officer like Generals Buhari, Mamman Vatsa, Magoro and many others. Where then did he get his wealth that his agents are defending that he was rich before he became the Head of State. Or was IBB in a different army from the one Generals Buhari and Mamman Vatsa were in? Agreed that it is said most of Nigerians have collective amnesia, but not when it comes to people who stole Nigeria dry and still flaunt this our stolen commonwealth scornfully in our face.

Ordinarily if IBB could stay quietly in his 50 bedroom hilltop house and enjoy his loot, we will definitely forget with time since time they say is the greatest healer. But it becomes annoying and irritating when he comes from his hibernation from time to time to add insult to the injury he had inflicted on us by insulting our collective intelligence.

Even children in primary schools in Nigeria and Ghana have been taught that Ibrahim Badamasi Babangida is the father of corruption in modern Nigeria. That he misappropriated $12.4 billion US dollars gulf war oil windfall. We are still wondering what his paid agents are defending.

Whatever Babangida and his paid agents say, Babangida has no moral or legal right to contest for any elective post in Nigeria anymore. By the singular act of annulling the June 12, 1993, he had sold his democratic right to participate in election. We know he has no conscience but we still remain him that the old legal adage which says "He who comes to equity must come with clean hands" and "He who wants equity must do equity." Let IBB ask himself whether he has passed these basic tests when it comes to his role in June 12 1993 election annulments. An apology can never be an atonement for June 12 annulment. What about the 40 or 400 billion Naira wasted on a fake transition project? What of the millions of those killed in the aftermath of the riot that followed that annulment? Criminal trial is the appropriate atonement. Any evil done by man will be redressed whether here or in the hereafter. This is my personal opinion.

APPENDIX XVII

The Evil Candidate: General Ibrahim Badamosi Babangida

Written by Naiwu Osahon Sunday
(Apart from Obasanjo, Babangida is the greatest evil ever to befall any country in the world)-All that Babangida, (nicknamed IBB), has to show for his over eight years in power in Nigeria, is private colossal wealth, and the edification of corruption in our body politics. Yes, he is richer than many African governments and can buy who ever he wants, but he ruined our lives to reach there. The book, The Sink, by Jeffrey Robinson, an American writer, says it all about Babangida. "Of the $120 billion siphoned out of the Nigerian treasury into offshore accounts by dishonest politicians, $20 billion is allegedly traceable to IBB directly as president from 1985 to 1993." The World Bank and other international sources of information put his total loot from the Nigerian treasury at over $35 billion.

He is now threatening to use a fraction of his loot to return to power and a figure of N400 billion has been mentioned by his cronies as his campaign chest. We ought to be worrying now about how to survive this viper's poisoned food. We are desperately hungry but if we eat, we die immediately. If we don't, we die slowly from hunger anyway, terrorized by the viper's fang. We are trapped. We can't get up to look elsewhere for food or do anything else. The evil genius has hijacked our destiny.

Fortunately, there are still principled, conscientious and patriotic Nigerians, determined that if they must die, it must not be without a fight. Babangida would not return to rule over one Nigeria. If he does, lovers of Nigeria would, at least, make Nigeria ungovernable for him, failing which, they would emigrate. I would definitely renounce my citizenship of Nigeria if nothing else.

The Yoruba have a proverb about: 'a person about to be roasted, who rubs his body with fat and goes to stand by a raging fire.' This must have influenced the following remarks on IBB by our popular human rights lawyer/activist, Mr. Femi Falana: "I am not quite sure that Nigerians can stop him from exposing himself to ridicule. He has been lucky that he is not in jail now. His coming out to contest will provide an opportunity for Nigerians to deal with him squarely and confront him with the annulment of June 12 election, the murder of Dele Giwa, and the Ejigbo tragic plane crash, the destruction of our values as a people, corruption, and massive violation of human rights." M. D. Yusufu, a former Inspector General of police said in Karl Maiers book, This House has fallen, that: "Babangida went all out to corrupt society. Abacha was intimidating people with fear. With him gone now you can recover. But this corruption remaings and it's very corrosive to society.

Professor Akin Oyebode of the University of Lagos law department describes IBB's attempt to return to power "as a colossal assault on the national psyche. At the end of the debate on the IMF conditionalities, he clamped on SAP, which was more draconian than the IMF conditionalities. Because he has a 50-bedroom house at Minna, he thinks the world is his oyster. He latches on the popular yearnings to launder his image. He has dirty rotten underwear that he wants to clean so that people will give him a new improved IBB. IBB is a bad statement to the whole world that at the end of the day we again brought Babangida to the scene. I don't want my children to live under Babangida. I won't live under Babangida." He does not even have the basic education or the intelligence. To be an expert at maneuvering a people and their treasury does not demonstrate intelligence as much as lack of moral fiber and self-discipline.

Babangida is an empty barrel midget, robed in threatening vulgar giant frippery of evil exploits. He lacks respect for democracy and worth of human life. He killed Dele Giwa. He closed down Ogun state radio; Concord, Guardian, Punch and Sketch newspapers; Newswatch and News magazines, during his time. He treated with contempt the Justice Chukwudifu Oputa led Human Rights Violation Investigation Commission (HRVIC), when summoned to answer charges on the murder of Dele Giwa. He also rushed to the court to prevent the implementation of the report of the Commission as it affected him.

Perhaps he wants to come back to rule so that he can retire with the biggest loot in history? But according to the book: The Sink, and International anti-corruption agencies reports, he has achieved that status already so why does he not want to leave us alone?

Speaking obliquely a few months ago in Babangidaspeak, he threatened that when he would speak on the June 12 annulment issue, Nigeria would shake to her foundations. In an interview in late May, 2004, on Channels TV, Babangida spoke on the June 12 issue, and no feathers were ruffled. Instead, Babangida admitted toothy smile and said, that he made a mistake and that he made it in the intrest of Nigeria. That was the same argument Mariam Abacha used when asked about her husband's loot stashed away in his foreign accounts. She said her husband was saving the money for Nigeria. On hindsight, we got some of the money back didn't we? That is more than can be said about Babangida's loot and the political turmoil he plunged Nigeria into since his selfish, irresponsible, June 12 annulment.

On why Babangida ignored all pleas not to kill Mamman Vasta, the master dribbler said that Vasta's death was a painful decision for him, but that he had no choice in the matter, because he was following military rules, and he did it in the national interest. But Vasta, his fellow infantry soldier and childhood friend, was hurriedly killed and his body dumped in a mass grave on the night of the announcement of his sentence, (i.e. early morning of 5th March 1986), to prevent last minute pleas for reprieve. Acid was poured on the bodies, including Vasta's and burnt, so one must ask, was the rush to kill Vasta and burn his carcass sanctioned too by the military laws? The whole thing smacks of envy, apart from being hideous and barbaric. Babangida used the phantom coup allegation to remove or marginalize the Middle Belt military top brass in his government.

Babangida said that he brought Obasanjo back to power to stabilize the polity. What he was not telling, was the apparent deal between the two of them not to probe each other in power. Otherwise, why would Obasanjo ignore the bigger rogues to vigorously pursue the return of Abacha's loot of a mere US$5 billion relatively?

Babangida on the Channels'TV interview said he wants to return to power to correct Nigerian problems because he has been there before. The man has no shame. Our most critical problem as a people is the rampant and systematic looting of our treasury by our successive leaders. Babangida was no exception, and he is being accused of the biggest loot of all, so, is he now saying that he wants to voluntarily refund whatever he is being accused of diverting from our coffers while in power? I have written personally to him before to do this, and he did not answer. He does not have to return to power to help Nigeria pay off her staggering foreign debt.

In a country of over 140 million people, what makes Babangida think he alone deserves to rule for perhaps seventeen or more years? What is he bringing to the table now if he never had it in the first place? Don't we deserve better than our past illiterate leaders who could not differentiate between the national and their private purses?

Of all the Nigerian military dictators, Babangida was the most desperate for power, and for attempting to hold on to it for life, apart from being the most flamboyant, cunning, callous, ruthless and deadly, about how they went about achieving their goals. Babangida grew on Nigeria slowly and quietly, with a deceptive toothy smile. Babangida first came into serious political reckoning with Buhari's misleading coup of December 31st 1983. In reality, power was seized for the opportunity to destroy documents relating to the NNPC's missing USA$2.8 billion oil money, and punish all those involved in the unraveling of the scam.

Politicians and critics, including Fela Anikulapo-Kuti, notorious for clamouring for the exposure of the oil money rogue Minister of an earlier military epoch, were locked up without trial. After consigning the vexatious matters that brought him to power to administrative oblivion with the help of Shinkafi, his Secret Service guru, Buhari announced his readiness to quit office. Idiagbon, as Buhari's lieutenant, naturally insisted on taking over as head of state from his apparently prematurely retiring boss. Babangida, who was Chief of Army Staff at the time and a member of the Supreme Military Council, insisted it was his turn to rule because he had been involved in virtually every military coup. The quarrel split the Supreme Military Council members almost equally behind the two principal combatants.

Akilu had just returned from a military training in India at the time and Babangida recommended him for appointment as the head of the Secret Service. Idiagbon by-passed Akilu and slighted Babangida by not consulting with him to confirm the new head of the Secret Service from the army.

Gloria Okon was arrested at the Murtala Mohammed Airport trying to smuggle cocaine out of the country. Gloria claimed to be a courier for the family of one of the two high ranking military officers deeply involved in the Supreme Military Council's palaver. Gloria was quickly smuggled out of the country and a carcass burnt beyond recognition of a human body, was left in her prison room to deceive the authorities. As Gloria's drama was playing out, Abiola brought a large consignment of banned newsprint into the country, forcing Idiagbon to insist on the arrest of Chief M.K.O Abiola.

All sorts of calamitous events kept rolling out at the time, including the arrest of one Ikuomola for trying to smuggle a large consignment of cocaine out of the country. He indicted a son of one of the Dantatas and they were both tried and sentenced to death. The Dantata family mounted pressure on the Supreme Military Council to commute the sentence to life. The issue heightened the division among the Supreme Military Council members, with the Gloria Okon's high ranking military benefactor, siding with Dantatas naturally.

Idiagbon insisted that if poor people found with cocaine could be punished with death sentence, why should the rich and affluent be spared? Idiagbon also wanted the lawyer, (a Rivers state chap who had received some four million naira as legal fees on the case at the time), to be shot along with the drug barons for benefiting from the evil.

The schism between Idiagbon and Babangida totally paralyzed the Supreme Military Council and it could no longer function. Idiagbon forced compulsory leave on Babangida, under close surveillance with tapped telephone lines and all. Chief M.K.O Abiola saw the opportunity to save his neck from the newsprint saga by teaming up with his friend, Babangida, and he provided the seed money for a coup.

Through the facilities of Abiola and the Dantatas, Yar Adua was brought into the picture to help influence the Saudi Arabian monarch to extend a special invitation to Idiagbon as a guest of the monarch, to perform the 1985 Lesser Hajj in Mecca. Idiagbon felt greatly honoured by the invitation and took with him to Mecca, most of his supporters on the splintered Supreme Military Council, including Mamman Vasta.

With Idiagbon (who was the head of the Buhari's regime in every sense of the word, and was very popular because of his transparent honesty, patriotism, and discipline), out of the way, Buhari (who was ready to vacate office anyway), was picked up like a helpless chicken at Doddan Barracks, and dumped in jail. Idiagbon, against the coupists' advice, returned home a people's hero, although locked up for several months too by Babangida.

The day after Babangida's coup, I attacked it on the front page of the Sunday Punch newspaper, as a ploy by the (IMF and the World Bank) to marginalize the naira and destroy our economy, and Babangida was described as a snake by nature and a stooge of the West. The Editor of the Sunday punch and his deputy at the time, Ayo Osintolu, and Bob Opone, respectively, were suspended from their jobs. Ayo for six months and Bob for three. I was unemployed as usual at the time, so, Babangida was handicapped about how to deal with me immediately. I heard later that I was blacklisted for all future government contracts and positions, even though my secondary school classmate Rear Admiral Aikhomu (rtd) eventually became Babangida's deputy in office. I never tried to find out.

Because of my reputation as someone you could persuade with superior argument but impossible to bribe out of his conviction, my best friend who was like a twin brother to me at the time, Com. Wole Bucknor (rtd), was detailed to plead with me to drop any further development of the IBB matter. Their strategy was to admit to me that my observations were absolutely correct but that Babangida meant well for Nigeria. With Babangida's antecedence, it was difficult for my friend to persuade me, but Nigerian newspapers in general at that early stage of the regime, were a little scared to publish and be damned.

Luckily, it did not take too long for Babangida to begin to reveal his secret agenda. He had removed Idiagbon/Buhari from power to douse the heated allegation at the time about illegal drug links and to help the IMF/World Bank ruin the naira and open up the Nigerian market as dumping ground for American and European junk and decadence. The marginalization of the naira suited Babangida's Machiavellian streak to blunt prospects of mass protests with abject poverty, hunger, and basic survival pre-occupations. For example, the terroristic power of massive foreign exchange loot in a private hand is limitless as a tool for forcing pauperized populace to acquiesce to the self- perpetuation antics of a potential despot.

Babangida's first pronouncement in power was to shock the nation by adopting the civilian title of president. He did this because of a secret personal ambition kept to himself, to transit into life president in the mould of Presidents Nasir of Egypt and Eyadema of Togo, and also because of his agreement to make Chief Abiola his Vice President for collaborating over their 1985 coup. Abacha kicked against Abiola becoming Vice President because he was eyeing Babangida's seat in a possible future coup of his own and wanted to remain the defacto next in command, in military terms, for eventual easy take over excuse.

Babangida promised Yar Adua a short-lived military transition after which he would hand over power to Yar Adua. That was why Yar Adua kept boasting during the early stages of Babangida's regime, that no force on earth could stop him becoming the next president of Nigeria. This prompted Obasanjo's statement at the time that Yar Adua must have forgotten something at the state house.

Babangida was so single minded, self-centered, and power-drunk, he single-handedly forced OIC membership on Nigeria without respect for our supposed religious secularity. He used every means imaginable to assert his power. Spiritual, criminal, everything was fair in his ruthless power game. The gods of the Marabouts became privileged guests at Aso Rock, lacing it with severe witchcraft, which was later vigorously sustained by Abacha.

Dr. T.C. Nwosu, the renowned Nigerian author, and I, came out in defense of Mamman Vasta, (when he was arrested for coup plotting), in a joint statement published as a news item at the time, in the Nigerian Guardian newspaper. We said it was a lie to accuse Vasta of trying to stage a coup to take the IMF conditionalities. This was the first time anyone, (civilian or military), would come out openly to defend an alleged coup plotter in Nigeria, and Vasta who was our friend and colleague in the Association of Nigerian Authors (ANA), took our support to heart, and arranged for some documents on his kangaroo trial for coup plotting to be smuggled out to us.

One of the documents we received was on Gloria Okon. We could not use the information in Nigeria at the time because no newspaper would dare publish it, so I arranged for Ejike Nwankwo, my bosom friend, to take the documents to his senior brother, Chief Arthur Nwankwo, who was in political exile in London at the time. The idea was for Arthur Nwankwo to have the Gloria Okon's story published in the Manchester Guardian, but Arthur decided to delay publication until he could use the immunity of the Nigerian Senate, which he was aspiring to join in Babangida's best time as a member, to make the story public. Senior members of the Ministry of Information, and of the Daily Times at the time, and a director of Newswatch, were not totally ignorant about what was going on in Babangida's government. In fact, Abacha at a point, asked the boss of the Ministry of Information to frame up Dele Giwa. The boss being a principled and die-hard journalist argued that it was difficult to frame up journalists.

Babangida's boys went ahead to frame up Giwa anyway. Three days before they killed Dele Giwa, Col. A. K. Togun, the deputy Director of Babangida's State Security Service (the SSS), invited Giwa to his office and accused him of involvement in the importation of arms while linking Giwa with other persons alleged to be trying to stage a socialist revolution in Nigeria. At the meeting, agreement was reached, and Babangida, through his emissaries, promised to meet Giwa's terms. Two days before Giwa's murder, Akilu allegedly phoned Giwa's home to ask for direction because Babangida's ADC "has Something for him, an invitation or something."

Dele Giwa allegedly invited the overseas editor of Newswatch at the time to be around. Obviously, Giwa took the president's promise more seriously than his colleagues at the Newswatch. This was why, when Giwa received the parcel and confirmed that it was from the President, his guest's first reaction was to dash off to take cover in the toilet adjacent to the room where Giwa opened the parcel bomb. The guest escaped death by the whiskers and blasted eardrums. Tagum, when asked by Airport Correspondents on October 27, 1986, about Giwa's bombing inadvertently confirmed the blackmail reason for Giwa's death when he said: "We came to a real agreement and one person cannot just come out and blackmail us. I am an expert on blackmail. If a motorcycle man suddenly dashed in front of a car and the driver kills the motorcycle man, another motorcycle man who was there would not say the motorcycle man who dashed in front of the car was wrong. He would say the driver killed him, not that he killed himself"

An Arab terrorist, who was recruited to collaborate with a University of Ibadan chemistry don especially for the task, produced the bomb. The terrorist is alleged to have gone with Major Buba Marwa, Ogbeha and Gwazo, in a Peugeot station wagon car with fake license plate numbers, to deliver the bomb at Dele's home. On arrival, they were told that Dele was not in, so they laid ambush near-by to watch movements in and out of Giwa's premises.

As soon as Giwa was spotted entering his house, the allegation continues, the Arab terrorist offered to go and deliver the bomb, but his colleagues in crime stopped him on the grounds that a white man would look too suspicious for the job. Marwa, accompanied by Ogbeha, are alleged to have delivered the bomb to Dele's son at the door, after which the crime team drove off to Mafoluku where they burned their delivery car. The same day, the Arab terrorist was flown out of Lagos, first to Kano, and eventually out of the country.

Major Buba Marwa was at the time rewarded with the rank of Lt. Col. and posted to the Nigerian Embassy in Washington, USA, as the new Military Attaché. His rise in the Army was extremely rapid and as Col. retuned home to be Governor of Lagos State. Armed robbers welcomed him to his new office with the kind of daredevilry never before experienced in Nigeria. Violence begets violence they say. The armed robbers raided from Mile two to Ikeja, even as he was passing by. Marwa panicked, so Babangida pumped unusual resources into Marwa's coffers to ensure his success, which is the genesis of his tramping around as an achiever today. His private life does not suggest that he suffered in fool's paradise.

Marwa, Ogbeha, and Gwazo, have since denied their alleged involvement in Dele Giwa's murder. Marwa, who now owns an airline and, therefore, knows that it takes less than eight hours to fly across the Atlantic to Nigeria, argued that he was studying in the USA at the time. The implication of this, of course, was that it was impossible to take a few days off his studies.

Marwa, who rose to fame through IBB's benevolence, is considered in military circles as one of the IBB boys, made up principally of the trusted cronies of the retired dictator. Accused of laundering money for IBB, Marwa again relied on the puerile argument that he was the Borno state governor in 1990, as if state governors are too busy governing diligently to travel out of Nigeria for a day or two, or even a week, on private businesses.

In December, 2005, when Marwa was detained for a couple of weeks by the EFCC, for laundering money for Abacha, he allegedly admitted that he had no choice in the matter as a military officer. He was only doing his duty. Of course, doing illegal duties loyally often goes with silencing, mouth-watering pecks, if nothing else.

As I said before, in the area of managing the national economy, Babangida bestowed his adroitness and moral degeneracy. His economy was dominated by male-wives, particularly in the banking and oil sectors. Women often brag about the efficacy of 'bottom' power. Feminine men sometimes flaunt it too as their passport to economic liberation. Between them and the suddenly very lucrative 419 business of the time, industry was complete. IBB's chiefs, allegedly colluded with 419 criminals to create the over-night semi-illiterate money-bags without class or shame, (including the 150 members of the National Assembly, that in 2005 sent IBB a birthday card), and who together now form the bulk of his supporters and campaigners, to return him to power.

Babangida (sapped) or totally wiped the middle class out of existence with the destruction of the naira, which he did by fiat in 1985, when he down graded the naira exchange rate from about N2 to N18 to the dollar. By the time he was forced out of office in 1993, the naira was exchanging at N60 to the dollar. Society was now reduced to two social classes of either the very poor or the rich rogues.

Babangida first concentrated on pulverizing his military base by tinkering with the 1985 Decree 17, to give himself sole authority to fire his military chiefs, including the chief of general staff; chairman, joint chiefs of staff;

service chiefs, and the inspector general of police. General Domkat Bali said at the time: "Babangida must have known what he was aiming at if you now take those powers of the President as civilian, and you now put them on any army officer who then sits with other army officers, in the name of Supreme Military Council, SMC, who are useless to him, whom he can change tomorrow, that means that name is not Supreme at all."

Bali was provoked to leave the government when he was demoted from the position of Minister of Defence to that of Internal Affairs. Ukiwe, a senior naval officer, who was IBB's deputy, was forced to retire even before Bali did, for demonstrating patriotic zeal in defense of team spirit, over our IOC membership saga.

Gideon Orkar's failed coup of April 22, 1990, provided Babangida with the opportunity to further purge the military. With total control over the military, IBB was ready to pursue his President-for-life agenda, (starting) by dismissing his S. J. Cookie's Political Bureau programme for the return to civil rule by 1990.

For over eight years, Babangida kept shifting his handing over date and juggling his transition programme by arbitrarily banning and unbanning politicians, particularly the known opponents of military rule. He spent N40 billion on his endless transition programme, and bribed all and sundry, including the NLC with N50 million, NUJ with N20 million, PMAN with N30 million, and so on, to try to silence them. He attempted to compromise some vocal critics by settling them, and those he could not recruit, he sacked where possible, or detained, or killed, or hounded into exile.

Less than two years into his rule in 1987, IBB announced that he was planning to bequeath a lasting legacy of civil rule, through a gradual learning political process. Four years into his regime in 1989, he lifted for the first time his ban on partisan politics, and set up two political parastatals. One was called the Social Democratic Party (SDP), and the other was the National Republican Convention (NRC).

The handing over date to civilian government was postponed once again from late 1990 to the 1st of October 1992. He allowed elections to be held into the local governments in 1990, and in 1991, Babangida instigated intra party squabbles to find excuse to ban 12 of the candidates participating in the governorship elections. Candidates replacing the disqualified ones had barely one week to campaign.

Elections into the State Assemblies miraculously held without too much acrimony, followed shortly afterwards by elections into the National Assembly. In all the elections, known individuals strongly against Babangida or the military in power were sidelined, banned, or hounded into exile, prominent among whom were Ibrahim Tahir of the NPN, Sam Mbakwe, Chris Okolie, Wahab Dosumu, Ebenezer Babatope, etc.

Government miraculously found the CBN documents when it suited it, and aspects of the documents concerning IBB, were published during the threat by members of the House of Representatives to impeach President Obasanjo in July, 2005, because of speculations that IBB was one of the Northern elites fanning the plot.

Babangida was ruthless in the way he amassed his colossal wealth. First is the illegal self-allocation of free oil, sold on the spot market. Then he initiated the corrupt culture of maintaining a huge monthly security vote virtually as personal pocket money. Rather than repair our refineries, let alone to work at maximum capacity, IBB built private refineries in Cote d'Ivoire and the Republic of Benin, where he took our crude to refine and sell back to us as fuel.

Perhaps you would want to join me to play the prude accountant, generous with figures. Let's pretend that Babangida was a General throughout his service years in the Nigerian army. Again let's assume he spent 30 years in the army and was paid N100,000 monthly (actually, salaries of Generals were less than N10,000 a month until recently) and he saved every kobo of his salary. He would be worth about N35,000,000 plus interest in the bank today. But Babangida's 50 bedroom palatial abode in Minna is alleged to be conservatively worth billions of naira and he does not owe any bank on it.

In 2003, he threw a wedding party for his first daughter, which numbed the nation. Some 28 governors were in attendance, and in June 2004, he treated us to another dream-like political carnival during his son's wedding. No one dared to ask where the money came from to set up such a palatial abode or scandalous and intimidating wedding carnivals in our jungle of abject poverty and hunger. Nigerians reveled in the lavish show of shame, hoodwinked by the audacity, the sumptuous food, the ambience, the vulgarity….. At least we saw our fellow Nigerians (albeit a handful of them), living it up on the money that could have guaranteed millions of Nigerians, active, regular employment indefinitely.

Babangida usurped eight years and eight months of the thirty-three years of military misrule and still wants to come back to finish us off properly. If he was honest with himself, he ought to be ashamed for the economic, political and social mess he has turned Nigeria into. Babangida should be heading for Kirikiri not Aso Rock.

Naiwu Osahon renowned author, philosopher of science, mystique, leader of the world Pan-African Movement.

APPENDIX XVIII

Corruption Inc.: The Halliburton List

Monday, April 19, 2010

That Nigeria has a 'punishment problem' is an understatement. Nigeria is unfortunately, a case study of how the rich and powerful use their influence to avoid punishment and successfully circumvent a justice system that is seen to benefit the well-connected. Given this reality, it is no surprise that the US Ambassador to Nigeria announced that the Halliburton scandal, in which many Nigerian officials have been fingered, is one that Nigeria could have tackled because it has all the information it needs.

SINCE 2003...

It was in 2003 when it was revealed that Kellogg Brown & Root, a company eventually acquired by international conglomerate Halliburton, gave approximately $180 million in bribes to Nigerian officials. By 2007, Halliburton admitted guilt and agreed to pay $492 million dollars in fines to the United States government for violating the Foreign Corrupt Practices Act.

A POSTURING HALLIBURTON PANEL

Despite the outcry from Nigerians demanding that the federal government bring to bear the Nigerians involved in the scandal; it was not until 2009 that the Yar'Adua administration created an investigative panel. The Panel was charged with naming those that benefited from the illegal Halliburton 'slush fund'. However, despite that panel's 8 week time limit and the fact that a year has passed, not one single individual has been named as promised by Yar'Adua.

AMERICA PUTS NIGERIA ON 'BLAST'

And now, adding more insult to the injury of all Nigerians, US Ambassador Robin Sanders specified on Wednesday, April 7th, 2010, that

*"[the] Nigerian government and ministers have ... enough information to act on their own as there are other countries that are involved and they have the same degree of access to those countries as we do. We know that that **information has been with the Nigerian government for quite sometime and with the previous ministers that have held that ministerial position**. So that information is there and is there for you to act on as your laws and your nation deems fit."*

CHECKMATE

According to the Vanguard newspaper, the Jonathan administration is set to finally release the long-awaited list of Nigerians tied to the Halliburton scandal. On the list are the following individuals -

1. Air Vice Marshal A. D. Bello (allegedly collected $15mn for a former dictator and himself)
2. Ibrahim Aliyu, (allegedly collected over $35mn for himself and a former dictator)
3. Abdukadir Abacha (allegedly collected $7mn)
4. Dan Etete (allegedly collected $3.5mn)
5. Jackson Gaius Obaseki (allegedly collected $11mn)
6. Gidado Bakare (allegedly collected $60mn for himself, a former dictator and some Northern elites)
7. Mark George (allegedly collected $6mn)
8. Ibrahim Babangida
9. Sani Abacha
10. Ernest Shonekan
11. Abdulsalami Abubakar
12. Rilwanu Lukman
13. Aliyu Gusau
14. Mariam Babangida (late wife of Ibrahim Babangida)
15. Miriam Abacha
16. Orji Kalu
17. Anthony Ukpo
18. Samuel Ewang
19. Aminu Saleh
20. Don Etiebet

It is worth noting that this list contains many political figures, dead and alive, that continue to play a role in Nigerian affairs. Ibrahim Babangida, for instance, plans to run for President in 2011 and Aliyu Gusau is the current National Security Adviser serving under acting President Jonathan. The names on the list reflect a truism, that most Nigerians know already - **the nation's political elite are tied to each other in corruption and only shed from their ranks when necessary for self-survival**. Consequently, one can only wonder what will happen if these names are formally released by the government. Will doing so put members of the current administration at risk, given that there must be others, yet to be fingered in this scandal who will do everything to preserve the status quo.

Irregardless, addressing this specific instance of corruption by identifying who took what will go a long way in getting Nigeria back on an anti-corruption track, something the current administration promised to do. Ultimately, those connected to the Halliburton scandal, must not be allowed to continue to benefit from the fruits of their corruption.

APPENDIX XIX

The Media in Babangida's Pocket
againstbabangida.com

The cream of the Nigerian press traveled to Minna to collect the dictator's bribe and feed the nation with his denial of established truth. Top journalists even presented Babangida with a birthday card, in total disregard for the canon of their profession. It was not a surprise, therefore, that the journalists allowed the former dictator, Ibrahim Babangida, to issue another of his boring denials at the restricted media parley, where they allegedly collected N10 million in "transportation money."

Saharareporters.com reports that the event started at 11 p.m. and ended just after 1 a.m. Among the editors and executives in attendance were Tunde Rahman and Ijeoma Nwogwugwu of ThisDay, Eze Anaba of Vanguard, Felix Abugu and Martins Oloja of the Guardian, Steve Nwosu of the Sun, Arowolo of The Punch, and Sam Omatseye of The Nation. Thisday Newspaper, photography director, Mr. Sumi Smart Cole, was the master of ceremony who presents the card.

Several sources told Sahara reporters that Ikeddy Isiguzo of Vanguard newspaper in Lagos was responsible for "mobilizing" the media executives and ensuring that they were friendly towards the general. But a source inside Babangida's disclosed that the former dictator's spokesman, Kassim Afegbua, afterwards had a tense exchange with Isiguzo whom he accused of allowing some of the media executives to "embarrass the general with tough questions." Our sources revealed that the general showed nervousness as some of the editors peppered him with hard questions. "It was not a comfortable atmosphere for General Babangida," said one source, adding that "Kassim later persuaded the editors not to use the question and answer exchanges but to focus on the general's statement."

The first four paragraphs of Babangida's prepared statement were devoted to praising the media. "It was the worst kind of hypocrisy," one of the media executives told Sahara reporters, adding, "as I watched the general try to massage our egos, it occurred to me that he must have thought that nobody in the room remembers how his regime abhorred the media." The source referred to Babangida's closure of several news outlets, including Punch, Concord, and News watch, his harassment or detention of numerous journalists, including New Breed publisher, Chris Okolie, and the culmination in the murder of Dele Giwa, one of the founders of News watch.

"I actually believe his speech was drafted by one or two of our colleagues who spent several days working with him underground," said our source.

In the speech, which served as a formal announcement of his presidential bid, Babangida claimed that he believes that the press has a role to play in his renewed but lackluster campaign to recapture power.

The former dictator's disjointed statement also touched on some of the issues that have nagged his widely unpopular, epileptic campaign. He spoke condescendingly about the annulment of the June 12 1993 election, stating that he had compensated for the annulment by supporting Mr. Olusegun Obasanjo to become president of Nigeria in 1999.

Mr. Babangida was sharply critical of those who have taken him to account over his widespread stealing and corruption that were documented in the Okigbo reports. He berated them as "misinformed critics," adding, "they have been using the Okigbo Panel Report in the most blindly controversial and distorted manner lacking fairness and morality."

One of our sources said that Babangida appeared visibly uneasy as he tried to deny that his regime was responsible for the death of Dele Giwa, one of Nigeria's foremost investigative journalists. "I could see the sides of his mouth twitch as he claimed that he believed in the sanctity of life.

Last week, two sources in Nigeria's military intelligence had told Sahara reporters that Babangida had plotted to eliminate General Mamman Vatsa and other innocent military officers by implicating them in phantom coup plots. Several years ago, the late Vatsa's family sponsored a documentary that revealed how Babangida plotted to eliminate Vatsa, a fine officer and poet.

Our sources, who are retired intelligence operatives, also stated that Babangida had contrived to down a military jet conveying many officers. One of the editors at the event said he cringed in embarrassment as Babangida said, "My discipline as a military commander also does not condone the killing of defenseless innocent people."

A source inside the campaign told Sahara reporters that Babangida was uncomfortable and looked tired throughout the parley claiming that it was because of the ongoing Ramadan fast. He added that the former dictator's handlers had gambled that, with the largesse offered to some of the media executives at the Minna parley, the retired general would start getting a more positive media coverage. The source said that Afegbua was irate with Isiguzo for doing a poor job of aligning some of the editors with the dreams of the campaign.

APPENDIX XX
Babangida's full statement:

Distinguished Gentlemen of the Press

TOGETHER, WE CAN BUILD OUR NATION

I am highly delighted by your kind response to my invitation for an interactive session with you on my political aspiration. I welcome you to my hometown of Minna and my residence. I believe this will be an open, frank and enriching interaction on the way forward for democracy in our great country. You are all key media players endowed with knowledge of Nigeria because of your primary preoccupation of being the watchdog of our society. I have written letters to a number of political leaders intimating them of my aspiration and I found it necessary to inform you in this interactive manner because the media as an institution plays a key role in educating, informing, reforming and entertaining the people.

It gives me great pleasure and utmost sense of comradeship to be in the midst of professionally eminent personalities of your pedigree who are the main pillars of our media industry that constitutes the entity called the "Fourth Estate" in our beloved country, Nigeria.

This fraternity with you today is neither a coincidence nor an accident. It is really a private platform for me to appreciate and elucidate my age-long reverence for the role of the press in modern civil society.

You are a beacon of hope, the shining torch of enlightenment, the amplifier of codified messages, agents of policy formulation and dissemination, the watchdog of democracy, molders of opinion and advocates of fundamental human rights. Truly, yours is no doubt a noble profession even though a thankless and hazardous one at that. I therefore wish to praise all media men, for your courage and commitment to national development.

The Press plays the key role of edifying and fortifying Democracy. The fact that your members have been able to hold the forte in the struggle for nation building without felling the apple cart, despite open assaults and risk to life, deserves kudos and accolades from all. May our country continue to flourish, so that your calling can develop more to enhance and advance our collective national dream! Together, we can build a strong, virile and prosperous Nigeria for unborn generations to behold and emulate.

I wish to acquaint your esteemed selves that my desire and interest to offer my stewardship by vying for the office of president in the 2011 general elections stemmed out of my belief and those of many other compatriots, that our country need an experienced and tested leader, who has a rich knowledge of the socio-economic and political dynamics of our people and country. Without being immodest, I have implicit confidence that I fit into that consideration.

Meanwhile, I believe you are aware of the robust debate as to whether or not I should contest the highest office in the land. In fact, some people in their negative criticism continue to render acrimonious misrepresentation to distort and disparage my true character and general contributions, past and present, towards the greatness of our dear country. Without sounding superfluous, from North to South, East to West, there are visible landmark achievements to underscore my contributions to national development and growth of our fatherland.

It behooves reason therefore to state that these diversions infringe upon my fundamental human right and democratic license to vote or to be voted for in an election. It is unjust and unfair to feign ignorance of this salient constitutional fact.

I have built bridges of understanding across our great nation, and held wide consultations and discussions with various classes of people on this project, with a view to charting a new developmental agenda for our dear country. Generally, the consensus has been the dire need for a dynamic, visionary, pragmatic, experienced, knowledgeable and detribalized leadership, to steer the ship of state and create opportunities for addressing contemporary challenges of nation building.

Given my wealth of experience and decades of leadership study, plus the urgent need to confront the challenges of our national lives, I believe the time is ripe for me to serve our people as a civilian president, with your kind support, cooperation and understanding. Thus, I intimate you formally of my studied decision to vie for the office of President in the 2011 general elections.

I believe that together we can drive the ship of state to the bay of hope and prosperity, through selfless service, positive political will and visionary leadership, based on skill and experience with consideration for national balance and effective separation of powers. My military discipline, knowledge of the country, democratization over the years, astute leadership endowments, amiability and nation-wide acceptance are eloquent testimonials for my qualification for the number one job. I say, like Sir Winston Churchill give me the tools and I will finish the job for you.

Permit me therefore to touch on some of the impressions and issues that you and I must have been confronted with relating to my personality and previous administration.

Why do I want to be President? Firstly, it is my constitutional right to do so. I have a fundamental right as a bona-fide Nigerian to vote and be voted for in an election. I am only exercising my franchise. Secondly, my previous government was a military one. I have seen over the years that many things could be done better. I have also spent many years to understudy democratic leadership in several countries and have mastered the art of democracy and learnt how to apply it better under our Nigerian conditions. History is replete with leaders who despite their ages, staged a come back. More than ever before, IBB is back with a lot of new policies that will drive Nigeria's plural society under a new federal system that will cater for the needs of the various nationalities for equity and unity. Additionally, we need to fix many things positively in our educational, infrastructural, energy, and economic, socio-political and moral lives. We must begin to address our minds on the practice of true federalism, creation of State Police to support our Federal Police, devise ways of running slim government, devolve power at the centre and build on our foreign policy and defense profiles. These are some of my attractions and motivation for leadership.

On June 12: Severally and with great remorse too, I have taken responsibility as a true leader for the actions and decisions of the military administration that I led. The annulment of the June 12 election is one of the ugly spots one has to live with. It was a collective decision taken after series of consultations with several stakeholders. Even though ours was a military regime, yet we governed as a team, majority decision always carried the day. I know that a day will come when Nigerians will forgive our regime because we are a godly nation that embraces the culture of forgiveness. After all, I introduced the era of new-breed politicians. In addition, the electoral formula we used is to date considered the most effective in the country. I am referring to "Option A4" and the establishment of two political parties. I am neither an enemy of democracy nor averse to the success of the candidates that contested the said elections. I knew both Bashorun MKO Abiola and Alhaji Bashir Tofa. Years after the annulment, I, in concert with other patriots, conscious of the geopolitical divides in the country, tried to assuage the feelings of the aggrieved people by supporting the candidacy of my senior military officer former President Olusegun Obasanjo, who in our estimation has an unshakeable faith in the unity of the country and who hails from the same State with Bashorun MKO Abiola.

OKIGBO REPORT: Many miss-informed critics have been using the Okigbo Panel Report in the most blindly, controversial and distorted manner lacking fairness and morality. They dwell so much on a purported $12.4billion Gulf Oil Windfall. Let me state categorically that the Okigbo Panel was never a trial court for me. The Federal Government set up the Okigbo Panel to examine the operations and make recommendations on the Re-organization of the Central Bank of Nigeria. Its scope of reference was from 1988-94, way beyond my tenure. It was not a probe of the Babangida regime but one aimed at improving the operations of the CBN. Kindly see details in the attached copy of a public announcement placed in the Vanguard of Thursday, June 10, 2010. The records are there for all to see. The Okigbo Panel made valued judgments on some items of expenditure funded with receipts into certain dedicated accounts. Nowhere did it indict me for any acts of financial impropriety. Throughout the panel's sitting, I was never subpoenaed.

ON DELE GIWA: For the umpteenth time, I wish to state that, I did not murder Dele Giwa. In addition, no agent or agency of government was found guilty of this heinous act by the law courts. I am a man of great faith in God and I believe in the sanctity of life. My discipline as a military commander also does not condone the killing of defenceless innocent people. Aside, court judgments have vindicated me on this. Some of them were by the esteemed Justice Candido Johnson who quashed the allegation for want of evidence by the prosecutors. Nevertheless, perception, often repeated, no matter how untrue, becomes very hard to obliterate.

Finally, my humble upbringing does not give room for one to join issues with juniors nor insult or disrespect elders. Better still, I do not quarrel with anyone, not even my peers. To all I accord mutual respect. I grew up with these ideals. However, a treasured attribute of mine has been grossly abused and misinterpreted by my critics. All thanks to Allah that my faith, Islam, is about a total submission to the will of the Almighty and abhorrence of oppression of others.

I guess you will find time in your quiet moments to reflect on these issues as you engage the public on a regular basis through your news report, articles, editorial comments and opinions. A formidable Press is surely the hub that wields together the tracking spokes in the wheel of national development. May your pens never run dry of indelible ink! On a lighter note, I think the press should also give our regime some credit for liberalising the space for the media, particularly the ownership of private television, radio stations and universities. God bless you all.

Long live Democracy.

Long live the Federal Republic of Nigeria.

HE IS SMART BUT ALWAYS ENDS UP BEING FOOLISH.

REFERENCES

I am indeed grateful to men of intellect whose materials I used in the compilation of this work, most of whom are not cited (kindly forgive me)- this might have been for security purpose or the fear of it, once more, I am sorry. I also wish to state categorically that the few I cited, especially those I mentioned their names, have no direct influence on this work, in fact, I don't know any of them.

http://:www. **fas.org,**

http://.sunnewsonline.com/webpages/opinion/2010/may/18/opinion-18-05-2010-002.htm
okey ndibe: Is Obama romancing Ibrahim Babangida?

http://www.saharareporters.com/letters/your-letters/6199-the-ibrahim-badamasi-babangida-saga.html

http://www.nairaland.com/nigeria/topic-22333.0.html#msg592409

http://www.punchng.com/Articl.aspx?theartic=Art200609052143979

http://www.saharareporters.com/index.php?option=com_content&view=article&id=4252:who-is-general-ibrahim-badamasi-babangida-the-evil-genius&catid=81:external-contrib&Itemid=300

http://www.nigerianbestforum.com/blog/?p=12910

http://www.nigerianbestforum.com/blog/?p=37126

http://www.leadershipnigeria.com/columns/views/interview/15391-ibb-is-in-the-race-for-good--aliyu

http://www.dawodu.com

http://www.nigeriancuriosity.com/2010/04/corruption-inc-halliburton-list.html

www.babangida.com

www.againstbabangida.com

www.ingramcontent.com/pod-product-compliance
Lightning Source LLC
Chambersburg PA
CBHW061407280526
45784CB00001B/396